Carol Ann Tomlinson and Jay McTighe

Integrating

& Differentiated Instruction

UNDERSTANDING *by* DESIGN

Connecting Content and Kids

Association for Supervision and
Curriculum Development
Alexandria, Virginia USA

®

Association for Supervision and Curriculum Development
1703 N. Beauregard St. • Alexandria, VA 22311-1714 USA
Phone: 800-933-2723 or 703-578-9600 • Fax: 703-575-5400
Web site: www.ascd.org • E-mail: member@ascd.org
Author guidelines: www.ascd.org/write

Gene R. Carter, *Executive Director*; Nancy Modrak, *Director of Publishing*; Julie Houtz, *Director of Book Editing &*
Production; Deborah Siegel, *Project Manager*; Reece Quiñones, *Senior Graphic Designer*; Keith Demmons, *Desktop*
Publishing Specialist; Vivian Coss, *Production Specialist*

All Web links in this book are correct as of the publication date below but may have become inactive or
otherwise modified since that time. If you notice a deactivated or changed link, please e-mail books@ascd.org
with the words "Link Update" in the subject line. In your message, please specify the Web link, the book title,
and the page number on which the link appears.

ASCD Member Book, No. FY06-04 (January 2006, PC). ASCD Member Books mail to Premium (P),
Comprehensive (C), and Regular (R) members on this schedule: Jan., PC; Feb., P; Apr., PCR; May, P; July, PC;
Aug., P; Sept., PCR; Nov., PC; Dec., P.

PAPERBACK ISBN-13: 978-1-4166-0284-2 • ASCD product #105004
PAPERBACK ISBN-10: 1-4166-0284-4
e-book editions: retail PDF ISBN-13: 978-1-4166-0376-4; retail PDF ISBN-10: 1-4166-0376-X • netLibrary
ISBN-13: 978-1-4166-0374-0; netLibrary ISBN-10: 1-4166-0374-3 • ebrary ISBN-13: 978-1-4166-0375-7;
ebrary ISBN-10: 1-4166-0375-1

Also available as an e-book through ebrary, netLibrary, and many online booksellers (see Books in Print for
the ISBNs).

Quantity discounts for the paperback book: 10–49 copies, 10%; 50+ copies, 15%; for 500 or more copies, call
800-933-2723, ext. 5634, or 703-575-5634.

Library of Congress Cataloging-in-Publication Data
Tomlinson, Carol A.
  Integrating differentiated instruction and understanding by design : connecting content and kids / Carol Ann
Tomlinson and Jay McTighe.
      p. cm.
  Includes bibliographical references and index.
  ISBN-13: 978-1-4166-0284-2 (alk. paper)
  ISBN-10: 1-4166-0284-4 (alk. paper)
  1. Teaching. 2. Learning. 3. Curriculum planning. 4. Individualized instruction. 5. Mixed ability grouping
in education. 6. Education--Research. I. McTighe, Jay. II. Title.

LB1027.3.T66 2006
371.102--dc22

10 09 08 07   12 11 10 9 8 7 6 5 4 3 2

Integrating
Differentiated Instruction
& Understanding *by* Design

PREFACE

Both authors of this book have worked on the ideas in it in one way or another for careers that now span well over three decades. Our particular personalities, experiences, talents, and predilections have led us to think about the varying and complementary facets of teaching and learning. We share a common attraction to classrooms. We have both been classroom teachers. We have both been administrators. We have both been teachers of teachers. Our professional paths have led us in different yet highly complementary and overlapping directions. We certainly have not come down these roads alone. Each of us has been nurtured by mentors, extended by professional partnerships, and challenged by minds that see further than we do—or differently.

Over the past nine years (give or take), we have each pursued a body of work that was born of our particular experiences and passions—and that continues to feed those passions as well. Tangible evidence of that work has emerged as ASCD has shepherded a series of books, videos, online courses, Web sites, and other tools for educators related to what we now call Understanding by Design (UbD) and Differentiated Instruction (DI).

We knew each other—and learned from each other's work. And we kept doing what busy people do. We worked diligently in the directions that we felt enhanced our work.

About four years ago, Sally Chapman from ASCD arranged a dinner for the two of us along with Grant Wiggins, Jay's colleague in UbD. The goal of the dinner was to explore the idea of a book or some sort of project that connected the two bodies of work on backward design and differentiation.

The dinner was good. We saw the logic of connecting the two models, and then we went back to busy lives and consuming agendas.

There was another dinner a year later—again at Sally's behest. We were again persuaded that her logic was sound and that the field would benefit from an explicit connection. After all, UbD and differentiation represent the elements of curriculum and instruction—the two halves of the classroom puzzle. The dinner was great. Our intentions for collaboration were sincere. We went home and again lost ourselves and our intentions in the tasks at hand.

Not easily dissuaded, Sally tried a different approach. She arranged for Jay, Grant, and Carol to present at an annual ASCD conference on the linkages between UbD and DI. That approach was concrete and inescapable. It required action.

The response from those in attendance was immediate and positive. "This is what we've been looking for," they told us. And they wanted more than we were prepared to give them.

Taking no chances on the future, Sally arranged a second joint presentation at a following ASCD conference, and with her ASCD colleagues Leslie Kiernan and Ann Cunningham-Morris, she began making longer-term plans for a UbD/DI collaboration (sometimes referred to as the UbDI project).

An ASCD summer conference linking UbD and DI was in the offing. The two ASCD professional development cadres that work with educators across the country and internationally to share ideas from the two bodies of work came together at ASCD to learn from one another about the two models and to shape the upcoming special conference—which would ultimately evolve to be more than a single event. Cannily, Sally and Leslie reserved a space in which Carol and Jay could work uninterrupted for a day to outline a book detailing the linkages between UbD and DI.

The rest of the story is predictable and plays out in the pages that follow. But it's not quite as straightforward as that. In the time intervening between the first dinner and the publication of this book, those of us who work with UbD and DI have been encouraged by the swell of interest in blending the two facets of educational practice. The questions we've been asked by practitioners about the linkages—and the role of UbD and DI in contemporary educational settings—have informed our work. Our colleagues have continued to push and refine our thinking. And we have benefited greatly from the "arranged marriage" of our ideas.

Our work is evidence of our belief that quality curriculum and instruction are—as they have always been—the bedrock of education and the avenue to developing thoughtful and fulfilled human beings. In addition, *skillful* instruction is an imperative in order to bring curriculum to life for young learners, and *flexible* instruction is necessary to make curriculum work for academically diverse student populations. Understanding by Design reflects our best professional understanding of curriculum. Differentiation reflects our best professional understanding of skilled and flexible instruction. High-quality learning should be the outcome of classrooms in which teachers consistently ask essential questions: "How can I get to know my students and their needs?" "What is most important and enduring for my students to learn about this topic?" "How can I ensure that each of my students learns as effectively and efficiently as possible?" "How will I know whether my students have learned what matters most?" As one expert explains, it takes robust curriculum and flexible instruction "if teachers are to have a realistic opportunity to meet the needs of all students in their classrooms, a truly daunting challenge given the increasing diversity of the student population" (Kameenui, Carnine, Dixon, Simmons, & Coyne, 2002, p. 27).

The linkage between UbD and DI is really that straightforward. The two models fuse to guide the professional growth of teachers who have the will to continue developing the skill necessary to answer those questions more fully through their practice. The book that follows examines the essential underpinnings of both models and demonstrates how the logic of each intersects with the other to promote classrooms that provide rich, durable, meaningful curriculum for the full range of learners that populate today's schools.

We are grateful to those who continue to work with us, those who are interested in our work, and those who hold our ideas to the fire. We'd like to think this book is just a step in a shared direction—for us, and for those who read what follows.

Acknowledgments

With appreciation and respect for our colleagues:

- the ASCD Understanding by Design Cadre: John Brown, Marcella Emberger, Judith Hilton, Everett Kline, Ken O'Connor, Elizabeth Rossini-Rutherford, Elliott Seif, Janie Smith, Joyce Tatum, Grant Wiggins, and Allison Zmuda; and
- the ASCD Differentiation Cadre: Karen Austin, Vera Blake, Kay Brimijoin, Deb Burns, Marcia Imbeau, Yvette Jackson, Sara Lampe, Carol O'Connor, Sandra Page, Judy Rex, and Nanci Smith.

Thank you for your partnership, dedication to quality, and capacity to bring insight and joy to our shared work.

1.

UbD and DI:
An Essential Partnership

What is the logic for joining the two models?
What are the big ideas of the models, and how do they look in action?

Understanding by Design and Differentiated Instruction are currently the subject of many educational conversations, both in the United States and abroad. Certainly part of the reason for the high level of interest in the two approaches to curriculum and teaching is their logical and practical appeal.

Beset by lists of content standards and accompanying "high-stakes" accountability tests, many educators sense that both teaching and learning have been redirected in ways that are potentially impoverishing for those who teach and those who learn. Educators need a model that acknowledges the centrality of standards but that also demonstrates how meaning and understanding can both emanate from and frame content standards so that young people develop powers of mind as well as accumulate an information base. For many educators, Understanding by Design addresses that need.

Simultaneously, teachers find it increasingly difficult to ignore the diversity of learners who populate their classrooms. Culture, race, language, economics, gender, experience, motivation to achieve, disability, advanced ability, personal interests, learning preferences, and presence or absence of an adult support system are just some of the factors that students bring to school with them in almost stunning variety. Few teachers find their work effective or satisfying when they simply "serve up" a curriculum—even an elegant one—to their students with no regard for their varied learning needs. For many educators, Differentiated Instruction offers a framework for addressing learner variance as a critical component of instructional planning.

That a convergence of the two models seems useful for addressing two of the greatest contemporary challenges for educators—crafting powerful curriculum in a standards-dominated era and ensuring academic success for the full spectrum of learners—is gratifying. The purpose of this book, however, is to move the conversations beyond a sense of "intuitive fit" to a more grounded exploration of why each of the models is potentially significant in today's classrooms—and why their partnership is not only reasonable but essential wherever teachers strive to help each student develop his or her maximum capacity.

With that goal in mind, we will first present a straightforward explanation of why the two models should be linked in the classroom. Then we will provide a set of axioms and corollaries that demonstrate important links between the two models. (Key theory and research that support UbD and DI can be found in the appendix.)

The Logic for Combining UbD and DI

Understanding by Design and Differentiated Instruction are not only mutually supportive of one another but in fact "need" one another. The reason is straightforward.

In effective classrooms, teachers consistently attend to at least four elements: whom they teach (students), where they teach (learning environment), what they teach (content), and how they teach (instruction). If teachers lose sight of any one of the elements and cease investing effort in it, the whole fabric of their work is damaged and the quality of learning impaired.

Understanding by Design focuses on what we teach and what assessment evidence we need to collect. Its *primary* goal is delineating and guiding application of sound principles of curriculum design. It also emphasizes how we teach, particularly ways of teaching for student understanding. Certainly the model addresses the need to teach so that students succeed, but the model speaks most fully about "what" and "how." In other words, Understanding by Design is predominantly (although not solely) a curriculum design model.

Differentiated Instruction focuses on whom we teach, where we teach, and how we teach. Its *primary* goal is ensuring that teachers focus on processes and procedures that ensure effective learning for varied individuals. Defensible models of differentiation will *necessarily* address the imperative of differentiating quality curriculum. Nonetheless, differentiation is predominantly (although not solely) an instructional design model.

If we had at our grasp the most elegant curriculum in the world and it missed the mark for students with learning disabilities, highly advanced learners, students with limited English proficiency, young people who lack economic support, kids who struggle to read, and a whole host of others, the curriculum would fall short of its promise.

On the other hand, if we were the most effective disciples of flexible grouping, interest-based instruction, responsive environments, and a host of instructional strategies that allow us to attend to learner variance but used those approaches in the absence of powerful curriculum, our classrooms would fail to equip students with the ideas and skills necessary to make their way in the world.

Simply put, quality classrooms evolve around powerful knowledge that works for each student. That is, they require quality curriculum and quality instruction. In tandem, UbD and DI provide structures, tools, and guidance for developing curriculum and instruction based on our current best understandings of teaching and learning.

That the two models stem from current best understandings of teaching and learning—and that they are not only compatible but complementary—will become more evident as the book progresses. At the outset of that exploration, it is useful to share some "axioms" and "corollaries" that demonstrate some ways the two models interface. The axioms are fundamental principles of Understanding by Design. The corollaries demonstrate the way in which Differentiated Instruction works to ensure that each student will have access to and support for success with the axioms. Together, the axioms and corollaries illustrate some ways in which UbD and DI work in tandem toward shared goals. For each set of axioms and corollaries, we'll provide a brief classroom scenario illustrating the combined logic of UbD and DI.

Axiom 1

The primary goal of quality curriculum design is to develop and deepen student understanding.

Corollaries for Axiom 1

• All students benefit from and are entitled to curriculum that develops and deepens their understanding.

• Given variance in student ability, experience, opportunity, language, interest, and adult support, they will grow at different rates and require varied support systems to develop and deepen their understanding.

Scenario

Mr. Axelt designs his curriculum around the essential knowledge, understanding, and skill reflected in both the subject he teaches and the content standards used in his district. Right now, his U.S. history students are studying the relationship between rights and responsibilities of citizens under the U.S. Constitution. He wants all of his students to explore the enduring understanding that democracies balance the rights and responsibilities of citizens who live in them. He also wants all his students to explore the essential question, "How are rights and responsibilities under the U.S. Constitution like and different from rights and responsibilities of members in other groups with which I'm connected?"

In Mr. Axelt's class of 32, he has three students with significant learning disabilities affecting their reading and writing. He has four students with a very advanced knowledge of U.S. history. He has several students who have great difficulty staying on task, some with identified learning problems and some who have no formal label. He has two English language learners. Some of his students have always liked history, and some have previously found it dull and disconnected from their lives. There's also a wide range of students' interests and learning preferences represented in his class.

Mr. Axelt begins teaching the unit on the U.S. Constitution with two primary goals in mind. First, he has designed tasks and assessments with the intent of having all his students understand the Constitution's essential principles and relate the principles to their own lives and experiences. Second, he is making instructional plans that use different materials, time frames, student groupings, and modes of student expression to ensure that each student will have fully supported opportunities to develop and extend the targeted understandings and skills.

Axiom 2

Evidence of student understanding is revealed when students apply (transfer) knowledge in authentic contexts.

Corollaries for Axiom 2

• Such authentic applications will reveal varying degrees of proficiency and sophistication in students' knowledge, understanding, and skill.

• The most effective teachers use the evidence of variance in student proficiency to provide opportunities and support to ensure that each student continues to develop and deepen knowledge, understanding, and skill from his or her current point of proficiency, interests, and learning preferences.

Scenario

Mr. Axelt's students will develop a charter for a group (family, team, class, club, etc.) that includes explicit and implicit indications of members' rights and responsibilities. Students will present their charter documents in a way that directly compares and contrasts their construction of rights and responsibilities with those concepts in the U.S. Constitution, and that makes a case for why their charter is at least as effective as the Constitution in addressing rights and responsibilities.

To provide for student variance in the class, students may select a group in which they have an interest for which they will develop the charter. To provide for student variance in reading sophistication, Mr. Axelt will work with the school media specialist to provide resource books and other materials, including bookmarked Web sites, at a broad range of reading levels. Students have the option of working alone on their charters or with a partner who shares an interest in the group for which the charter will be designed and a preference for collaboration. Mr. Axelt will also offer brief minisessions on various facets of the charter design and reflection process for students who want that extra support and guidance.

Axiom 3

Effective curriculum development following the principles of backward design (described in Chapter 3 and explored throughout the book) helps avoid the twin problems of textbook coverage and activity-oriented teaching in which no clear priorities and purposes are apparent.

Corollaries for Axiom 3

• *All* learners benefit from and should receive instruction that reflects clarity about purposes and priorities of content.

• Struggling learners require focus on the truly essential knowledge, understanding, and skill of a unit to ensure that their efforts are most efficient and potent in moving them forward in reliable ways.

• Advanced learners need challenge predicated on what is essential in a discipline so that their time is accorded value and their strengths are developed in ways that move them consistently toward expertise in the disciplines.

Scenario

Activities, discussions, and assessments in Mr. Axelt's class are designed to ensure that all students focus on the unit's enduring knowledge, understanding, and skills. He also uses the essential knowledge, understanding, and skill as a focal point for differentiating instruction for students who struggle to learn and for students who are advanced as learners.

Mr. Axelt's students who struggle to learn and have gaps in prior knowledge and skill still focus on the enduring understandings and skills of the unit. Mr. Axelt makes opportunities to work with students on skills they are lacking and often asks them to apply those skills to their assessment tasks. For some of these students, he may emphasize important skills and knowledge from past years rather than "nice but not imperative to know" knowledge and skill from the current unit. Whatever adaptations he makes for these students, however, their focus on the unit's enduring understandings and skills remains a constant in his planning for them.

When Mr. Axelt has evidence that students have already achieved proficiency with unit goals, he recrafts homework, sense-making activities, and key assessments to provide appropriate challenge as well as opportunity for these students to pursue interests. The adaptations continue to focus students on the unit's enduring understandings—but at a level of greater sophistication than is currently appropriate for other students.

Axiom 4

Regular reviews of curriculum and assessment designs, based on design standards, provide quality control and inform needed adjustments. Regular reviews of "results" (i.e., student achievement) should be followed by needed adjustments to curriculum and instruction.

Corollaries to Axiom 4

• Results of reviews will inevitably show variation among students in essential knowledge, understanding, and skills.

• Results-based adjustments to curriculum and instruction should be targeted to the individual as well as to the class as a whole.

• Results-based adjustments will require flexible use of time, teacher attention, materials, student groupings, and other classroom elements to ensure continued development and deepening of students' understanding.

Scenario

Mr. Axelt preassessed his students to determine their points of entry into the unit and also surveyed them regarding particular interests related to the unit. When he saw that some students already demonstrated detailed understanding of the unit's enduring understandings, he used the assessment results to think about alternative learning routes for these students. Similarly, when preassessment results suggested gaps in precursor skills and understandings for some students, he planned small-group instructional sessions and some alternate homework assignments to address these needs.

As the unit progressed, Mr. Axelt used formative or ongoing assessments to chart the progress of his students, continuing to develop small-group and individual learning plans for students who needed additional instruction and exploration in a given area and for students ready to move ahead.

This week, Mr. Axelt divided class time into thirds. He spent about a third of the class time working with all students to contrast the perspectives of various citizen groups on rights and responsibilities related to the First Amendment. He allocated about a third of class time to have students develop oral or written responses from a group of citizens to the balance of rights and responsibilities related to the Second Amendment. The final third of the class time he allotted to instruction of small groups assembled on the basis of need for work with research and writing skills, as indicated by the unit preassessment and reflection on the students' previous key assessment task.

During the direct instruction portions of the week, he presented ideas and information to the whole class, illustrated use of key skills, and engaged students in small- and whole-group consideration of one of the unit's key questions. During student sense-making time, he met with students in small groups for specific needs and moved among students to view and take notes on their work and to coach them as they worked.

Axiom 5

Teachers provide opportunities for students to explore, interpret, apply, shift perspectives, empathize, and self-assess. These six facets provide conceptual lenses through which student understanding is assessed.

Corollaries to Axiom 5

• All students should be guided and supported in thinking in complex ways.

• It is *not* the case that struggling learners must master the basics before they can engage in thinking. Rather, evidence clearly suggests that for most students, mastery and understanding come through, not after, meaningful interaction with ideas.

• Nonetheless, students will differ in the level of sophistication of their thinking and understanding at a given time.

• Teachers should be prepared to provide opportunity and support to continually develop students' understandings and capacities as thinkers.

Scenario

In the current lesson, students are examining varied contemporary perspectives in the United States on a citizen's rights and responsibilities under the Second Amendment. Mr. Axelt provided all students with three key questions to guide their thinking about the issue. Students could select a "constituency group" (e.g., law enforcement officers, hunters, a neighborhood watch group, gun manufacturers) whose perspective they are interested in investigating.

Students who have a need for support with vocabulary received a key vocabulary list of essential words and clear explanations of the words. Students who need structure in gathering data worked with a graphic organizer designed to help them categorize ideas they found. Mr. Axelt also designated resource materials at various levels of difficulty. Students could select resources designated as "straight ahead," "uphill," and "mountainous." Students are accustomed to such designations (which vary from time to time in number of options and language used to describe them) and generally select resources appropriate for them. When they err, he coaches them individually to analyze their choices.

At the end of the lesson, students will meet in groups of four with members representing at least three perspectives on the topic. The groups will receive questions to guide their small-group discussions. They will then respond individually in their learning logs to a question designed to probe their thinking on how and why people's perspectives vary widely on issues like gun control. The learning log entries provide formative assessment data to guide the teacher's instructional planning as the unit moves ahead.

Axiom 6

Teachers, students, and districts benefit by "working smarter" and using technology and other vehicles to collaboratively design, share, and critique units of study.

Corollaries to Axiom 6

• Students also benefit when teachers share understandings about students' learning needs, classroom routines, and instructional approaches to ensure that each student develops knowledge, understanding, and skills as fully as possible.

• A routine part of collaboration in academically diverse classrooms should occur between teachers and specialists who have expert knowledge about student needs and instructional approaches most likely to respond effectively to those needs.

• Technology should be used to address varied learner needs and to assist the teacher in keeping track of student growth toward important curricular goals.

Scenario

Mr. Axelt and his departmental colleagues have designed their curriculum together and meet periodically to evaluate its effectiveness, suggest modifications for future consideration, and share resources. They also discuss issues related to working in responsive classrooms. Teachers find that their varied perspectives and experiences are complementary and nearly always result in worthwhile suggestions for both curriculum and instruction. Of particular importance in these meetings is the presence of specialists who can make suggestions for differentiating unit plans for various needs—such as students who need to move around to learn, students who need reading support, students who need to work at advanced levels of challenge, and so on. Over time, the resource teachers have helped their colleagues develop a repertoire of strategies such as think-alouds, paired reading, learning contracts, compacting, expert groups, and varied modalities of exploring and expressing ideas.

Axiom 7

UbD is a way of thinking, not a program. Educators adapt its tools and materials with the goal of promoting better student understanding.

Corollaries to Axiom 7

• Differentiated instruction is a way of thinking, not a formula or recipe. Educators draw on, apply, and adapt its tools with the goal of maximizing knowledge, understanding, and skill for the full range of learners.

• Effective differentiation guides educators in thinking effectively about whom they teach, where they teach, and how they teach in order to ensure that what they teach provides each student with maximum power as a learner.

Scenario

Mr. Axelt sees himself as a learner. He is guided in his professional growth by principles of curriculum design and instructional responsiveness, but he understands that those principles are guidelines, not straightjackets. He realizes that he is like his students in needing to develop clarity about the intent of the guiding principles, but that his understanding of them will continue to deepen through each cycle of teaching a unit and each encounter with students. He continues to ask himself, "What does it mean for my students to understand this topic in ways that are relevant, are authentic, and give them power as learners?" and "What can I do to make sure each of my learners is fully supported in growing as fast and as far as possible in understanding this topic?"

Professionals in any field are distinguished by two characteristics: (1) They act on the most current knowledge that defines the field, and (2) they are client centered and adapt to meet the needs of individuals. As the book progresses, we hope you will come to see more clearly the role of Understanding by Design in ensuring that educators identify and teach the essential knowledge, skills, and enduring understandings that shape each of the disciplines and the role of Differentiated Instruction in making certain that each learner has maximum opportunity to benefit from high-quality experiences with those essentials—and their complementary roles in doing so.

2

WHAT REALLY MATTERS IN TEACHING? (THE STUDENTS)

How can students' lives influence their classroom experiences?
Why does it matter to teach responsively?
What are some starting points for responsive teaching?

At its core, teaching is an art that calls on its practitioners to work simultaneously in multiple media, with multiple elements. Central to teaching is *what* we ought to teach—what we want students to know, understand, and be able to do. To be an expert teacher is to continually seek a deeper understanding of the essence of a subject, to increasingly grasp its wisdom. That understanding is key to a teacher's role in curriculum planning. It is difficult to imagine someone becoming a great teacher without persistent attention to that element of the art of teaching. We'll examine the centrality of the role of curriculum design in the practice of artful teaching in Chapter 3.

A second medium or element central to the art of teaching is the student—*whom* we teach. The student is the focal point of our work as teachers. We believe the lives of students should be shaped in dramatically better ways because of the power and wisdom revealed through high-quality curriculum. In a less complex—less human—world, teaching might simply be telling young people what's important to know. In such a setting, students would say, "I see. Thanks." And the world would go forward.

But human beings *are* varied and complex. The varieties and complexities demand every bit as much study from the teacher as does curriculum content. Failure to attend to that requirement is likely to result in failure of the teaching enterprise for many, if not all, students. Before the curriculum design process begins, as it progresses, and as curriculum is tested and refined in classroom practice, the best teachers are mindful that teaching is judged by successful learning and that learners will inevitably and appropriately influence the effectiveness of the art we practice. The goal of this chapter is to provide a brief exploration of some ways in which learner variance shapes the art of teaching. We have elected to begin our discussion of UbD and DI with a focus on students as a way to affirm our belief that students should always be in the forefront of our thinking as we make, implement, and reflect on our professional plans.

Some Cases in Point

Each year, teachers enter their classrooms with a sense of direction provided by some combination of personal knowledge of subject matter, content standards, and teaching materials. As teachers become more experienced, they develop a refined sense of how the journey ahead will unfold in terms of time, benchmarks for progress, and particular routes of travel, fully mindful of the needs and interests of learners. Each year, students reinforce for those teachers that the journey is a shared endeavor and that the best-laid plans of the best teachers are just that—plans, subject to change.

A Personal Barrier to Learning

Elise, a previously strong student, was failing every test, missing assignments. She was not progressing academically, and her teacher knew it. She talked with Elise and with her mom on many occasions. Elise was nonplussed. Her mom was surprised. She promised support from home—and provided it. Elise ended the year with a D in the class. An F was within easy reach. Months more passed before the mystery of why she was heading steadily downhill was solved. Elise's parents had separated just as the school year began. Although she could not have articulated the plan clearly, Elise was operating with the belief that if she performed poorly in school, her parents would have to get together to address the problem. If her failures persisted, so would the parental conversations. In the end, she tenaciously believed, they would reunite. A student's personal crisis eclipsed the teacher's well-developed plans.

Identity as a Barrier to Achievement

Jason was an amazing contributor to group plans in class and to class discussions, but his individual performance was mediocre at best. He began work far more often than he completed it. Homework rarely came in on time, if at all. He was sometimes contentious in class—especially toward the teacher, to whom, at other times, he seemed to relate in a very positive way.

In a conversation with the principal later in the year, Jason flared. "When you understand what it's like to be the only kid on the bus who wants to do homework, what it costs to study after school instead of shooting hoops, *then* you tell me how to live my life!" Jason, an early adolescent, was struggling with issues of race and academic identity. The struggle was "loud" in his mind, drowning out the curriculum just as it was complicating his view of his teacher.

A Learning Problem as Obstruction

Yana hated writing more fervently with each assignment. Normally happy and good spirited, she could not contain tears when faced with a writing deadline. The teacher's first attempt to deal with Yana's frustration was to extend the deadline for Yana when she had no paper to turn in at the designated time. That resulted in a multipage paper that seemed to have no beginning, middle, end, or discernible intent. Multiple conversations with Yana yielded multiple approaches to solving her undefined problem—all unsuccessful.

Then one day, the teacher discovered that Yana could explain with power and conviction the ideas that turned to mush in writing. On instinct, the teacher cut Yana's essay into "thoughts"—ideas that made sense as a unit, but not in sequence. She said to Yana, "Now, put the strips in order the way you'd tell them to me." Through tears, Yana found she was able to make sense of the jumble of ideas in that way. The approach not only opened up new possibilities for writing success for Yana but also resulted in diagnosis of a previously undiagnosed learning disability. To get to a point of productivity, the teacher had to let go of a planned sequence of assignments and work with one task until she and the student could unravel a problem that was blocking the student's progress as a writer.

An Idiosyncratic Learning Need Inhibits Achievement

Noah was generally a delightful kid who had been deemed "bad" for the past couple of years. He seemed unable to stay still in the classrooms of several teachers who valued stillness as a prime virtue in students. The more he was scolded for moving at "inappropriate" times, the more he moved inappropriately. In this year's class, Noah was fine. When he got deeply involved in an idea or discussion, he got up and paced around his desk, but no one seemed to care. In fact, his teacher came to see Noah's movement as an indicator of the energy in a class period. One day as he paced while working on an assignment, he said to no one in particular, "I think I learn better when I move. That's cool to know, isn't it?" Noah was, in fact, a highly kinesthetic learner in a world that often honors sitting still. For him, mental energy exhibited itself through physical energy. When his way of learning became acceptable, he became a better learner.

These students are not an author's creation. They are real students in real classrooms. Their teachers invested time, care, and mental energy in crafting curricula that complemented their belief in the possibilities of each student and the role of knowledge in helping students achieve their potential. Nonetheless, the students were actors in the classroom drama—every bit as potent as the teacher and the curriculum. The unique lives of the students significantly shaped their experience with and response to school. When a student need took center stage, it became necessary for the teacher to adapt the "script" to account for that need. In two instances the teacher found a way to address the learner's particular needs. In the other two, the year ended with their problems still intact. It is, of course, the optimism of teaching that if we keep trying, we will find a way to address problems that, in the meantime, obstruct learner success.

Students Are Much Alike—and Very Different

Elise, Yana, Jason, and Noah are much like all other students. They came to school not so much seeking mastery of geometry and proficiency in paragraph writing as seeking themselves. That is, like all humans, they are looking for a sense of their own meanings, roles, and possibilities. They come wanting to make sense of the world around them and their place in that world.

Toward that end, they come to the classroom first looking for things like affirmation, affiliation, accomplishment, and autonomy (Tomlinson, 2003). They are looking for adults who accept them, value them, guide them, and represent for them what it means to be a competent and caring adult. Quality curriculum should play a central role in meeting the core needs of students for affirmation, affiliation, accomplishment, and autonomy, but it is the teachers' job to make the link between the basic human needs of students and curriculum. Although the physical, mental, and emotional characteristics of students vary between kindergarten and high school, their basic needs as learners and as human beings do not. These basic needs continue to govern what young people look for in schools and classrooms.

Similarities notwithstanding, however, young people differ—sometimes remarkably—in the ways that they experience the quest for self and meaning. In fact, it is the differences young people bring to school with them that shape how they come to see themselves in the context of curriculum and school.

There are many ways to think about how student variance shapes students' school experiences. A teacher who arrives in the classroom with elegant curriculum is likely to stand before students of advanced ability and students who come trailing disabilities, students from poverty and students from plenty, students who dream bold dreams and students who do not believe dreams are worth their time, students who speak the language of power and students to whom that language is unfamiliar, students who learn by listening and those who learn through application, students who are compliant and those who challenge authority on every hand, students who trust and those who are damaged and devoid of trust. To pretend those differences do not matter in the teaching/learning process is to live an illusion. Figure 2.1 presents a few possible categories of student variance, elements shaping those categories, and some implications for learning.

It is regrettably often the case that, as teachers, we identify those students whose attributes are a good fit for the structures of our classrooms and pronounce them "successful," while assigning other students to the category

FIGURE 2.1

Some Categories of Student Variance with Contributors and Implications for Learning

Category of Student Variance	Contributors to the Category	Some Implications for Learning
Biology	Gender Neurological "wiring" for learning Abilities Disabilities Development	High ability and disability exist in a whole range of endeavors. Students will learn in different modes. Students will learn on different timetables. Some parameters for learning are somewhat defined, but are malleable with appropriate context and support.
Degree of privilege	Economic status Race Culture Support system Language Experience	Students from low economic backgrounds, and representing races, cultures, and languages not in positions of power, face greater school challenges. Quality of students' adult support system influences learning. Breadth/depth of student experience influence learning.
Positioning for learning	Adult models Trust Self-concept Motivation Temperament Interpersonal skills	Parents who actively commend education positively affect their children's learning. Trust, positive self-concept, positive temperament, and motivation to learn positively impact student learning. Positive interpersonal skills and "emotional intelligence" positively impact student learning.
Preferences	Interests Learning preferences Preferences for individuals	Student interests will vary across topics and subjects. Students will vary in preference for how to take in and demonstrate knowledge. Students will relate to teachers differently.

of the "unsuccessful." In truth, far more students would be successful in school if we understood it to be our jobs to craft circumstances that lead to success rather than letting circumstance take its course. Even the best curriculum delivered in a take-it-or-leave-it fashion will be taken by a few and left by too many.

Why It Matters to Teach Responsively

Responsive or differentiated teaching means a teacher is as attuned to students' varied learning needs as to the requirements of a thoughtful and well-articulated curriculum. Responsive teaching suggests a teacher will make modifications in how students get access to important ideas and skills, in ways that students make sense of and demonstrate essential ideas and skills, and in the learning environment—all with an eye to supporting maximum success for each learner. Responsive teaching necessitates that a teacher work continuously to establish a positive relationship with individual learners and come to understand which approaches to learning are most effective for various learners. Learner success benefits from teachers who are responsive to a learner's particular needs for numerous reasons:

• **Attending to teacher–student relationships contributes to student energy for learning.** Beyond the potent benefits of human beings learning to understand and appreciate one another, positive teacher–student relationships are a segue to student motivation to learn. A learner's conviction that he or she is valued by a teacher becomes a potent invitation to take the risk implicit in the learning process.

• **Attending to the learning environment builds a context for learning.** When students feel affirmation, affiliation, a sense of contribution, growing autonomy, accomplishment, and shared responsibility for the welfare of the group, the "climate" for learning is good. Such a climate does not guarantee student success, but it opens the way and provides a setting in which consistent partnerships help students navigate success and failure as a part of human growth.

• **Attending to students' backgrounds and needs builds bridges that connect learners and important content.** Such connections contribute to relevance for students—an important attribute of student engagement.

- **Attending to student readiness allows for academic growth.** Our learning expands when the work we do is a little too difficult for us and when a support system exists to get us past the difficulty. Because students' readiness to learn particular ideas and skills at particular times will inevitably vary, a teacher must make appropriate readiness adjustments to enable consistent academic growth for each learner.

- **Attending to student interest enlists student motivation.** Learners of all ages are drawn to and willing to invest in that which interests them. Interest ignites motivation to learn. A teacher who makes consistent efforts to pique a student's curiosity, discover students' particular and shared interests, and show students how important ideas and skills connect to their interests is likely to find students who are far more eager and willing to learn than they would be if they found content and skill to be remote from their interests.

- **Attending to student learning profiles enables efficiency of learning.** Enabling students to work in a preferred learning mode simply "unencumbers" the learning process. When learning challenges are already substantial, it is sensible to allow students to work in ways that best suit them.

In all classrooms, it is important for teachers to ask, "Can I afford to sacrifice student trust and buy-in, growth, motivation, or efficiency of learning?" To the degree that a high level of learning for each student is the teacher's goal, the answer to the question must certainly be that these student attributes are imperatives. Student learning will diminish in direct proportion to teacher inattention to any of the attributes.

Basic Approaches to Responsive Teaching

Differentiation does not advocate "individualization." It is overwhelming to think that it might be the teacher's job to understand fully the needs of every single student, including those from a wide range of cultural and language groups, who struggle to read or write, who grapple with behavior challenges, who are advanced in performance, who come to us from oppressive home settings, and so on. Feasibility suggests that classroom teachers can work to the benefit of many more students by implementing *patterns* of instruction likely to serve multiple needs. Beyond that, it's always desirable to study individuals in order to make refinements in the teaching patterns. But implementing patterns and procedures likely to benefit students who have similar needs (while avoiding labeling) is a great starting point. Consider the following 10 teaching patterns that cut across "categories" of students and benefit academic success for many learners.

• **Find ways to get to know students more intentionally and regularly.** For example, stand at the classroom door and address the students by name as they come and go, use dialogue journals through which students have an opportunity to establish a written conversation with you, and take observational notes when students are discussing or working. These and many other approaches are effective in getting to know students, even when there are "too many of them." Such approaches also convey messages to students that they matter to teachers.

• **Incorporate small-group teaching into daily or weekly teaching routines.** Once a teacher and students become accustomed to procedures that allow some students to work independently (or in small groups) while the teacher works with a few students, the door is open for the teacher to target instruction on a regular basis to students who need to be taught in different ways, students who need assistance with basic skills, students who need to hear competent readers read aloud or who need "safe" opportunities to read aloud, students who need to be pushed further than grade-level expectations, and so on. Again, students seldom miss the point that a teacher is trying to help them succeed.

• **Learn to teach to the high end.** Studying and implementing strategies for extending learning of highly able students has many benefits. Most obvious among them is providing challenges for students who are often left to fend for themselves in finding challenges. However, the vast majority of students would benefit from tasks designed to foster complex and creative thinking, support for increased independence, self-assessment, metacognition, flexible pacing, and so on. The best differentiation inevitably begins with what we might assume are "too high expectations" for many students and continues with building supports to enable more and more of those students to succeed at very high levels.

• **Offer more ways to explore and express learning.** Many learners would benefit from routine opportunities to make sense of ideas through analytical, creative, or practical avenues, for example. Many learners would benefit from assignments and assessments that remain staunchly focused on essential learning outcomes but allow them to express their learning in ways that best suit their strengths and interests through varied products and performances (e.g., writing, speaking, acting, or visually representing).

• **Regularly use informal assessments to monitor student understanding.** For example, have students answer one or two key questions on an index card as a class period ends and turn the card in to the teacher at the end of the class period. Such an approach can help a teacher sense which individuals have mastered an idea or skill, which individuals hold misconceptions, which are still at the starting block of proficiency, and which individuals need extra support to become proficient. Such "exit cards" are not graded; they simply provide a snapshot that allows more targeted instructional planning for the days ahead.

• **Teach in multiple ways.** Use part-to-whole and whole-to-part explanations. Use both words and images. Model or demonstrate ideas. Use examples, stories, analogies, and illustrations derived from students' experiences. A teacher who regularly presents in these varied modes is likely to reach far more students than one who "specializes" in one mode.

• **Use basic reading strategies throughout the curriculum.** A teacher who regularly uses "read-alouds," "close reads," "split entry comprehension journals," and related mechanisms helps many students read with greater purpose and comprehension.

• **Allow working alone or with peers.** Many times, it makes little difference to the day's content goals whether students work independently or collaboratively on a task. Giving students the option (within required behavioral parameters) can improve learning for many students with both preferences.

• **Use clear rubrics that coach for quality.** Sometimes classroom rubrics resemble "bean counters"; for example, if a student does four of something, it's deemed to be better than three. Such rubrics do little to provide specific guidance or support metacognition about quality work and work habits. Rubrics that clearly explain the traits of "good" work and move up from there can coach far more students in progressing from good to exemplary. In addition, the rubrics can provide space for students to add personal goals for success or space for the teacher to add a student-specific goal.

• **Cultivate a taste for diversity.** Schools and classrooms often seem structured in ways that squelch diversity and lead not only to a poverty of thought but to a poverty of opportunity as well. Pose questions that can be answered from multiple vantage points, and make it safe for students to express diverse views. Ask students to find multiple ways to solve math problems. Encourage groups of students with very different talents to find varied ways to express understandings. Invite students to suggest ways they might structure the classroom, and draw on the approaches. Learn about the cultures of your students, and study the impact of race on students and learning. Consistently use examples, illustrations, and materials related to varied cultures. Ask students to compare idioms, ways of celebrating important events, heroes, stories, and so on, from their backgrounds. As a colleague reminded us, it's important not to mistake the edge of one's rut for the horizon. Our world—and our students'—is much expanded by seeing possibilities through many different eyes.

It's not necessary to implement all of these possibilities to begin being a more responsive teacher. It does matter to begin finding ways to become more aware of individual learners, to make the classroom more generous in reaching out to an array of learners with a sense of high possibility, and to develop varied pathways of teaching and learning so that the potentials of many different learners can be realized.

Beginning at the Beginning

Excellent teaching is of immense importance. So is coherent, meaning-rich curriculum. But in the end, education is about learning. Learning happens *within* students, not *to* them. Learning is a process of making meaning that happens one student at a time. Even as we begin consideration of the kind of curriculum most likely to support students in developing enduring understandings and powerful skills, we have to acknowledge that however impressive our curriculum design, it will have to be implemented in diverse ways according to diverse timetables and in response to diverse learner needs—or else it will not result in the learning for which we cast our plans.

Thus, always in our minds as we design curriculum must be these questions: Whom am I preparing to teach? How can I bring knowledge of my students to bear on the way in which I design curriculum? How can I help these particular students find themselves and their world in what I am about to teach? Then as we design and implement the curriculum, we need to continue asking: How might I teach in ways that best reveal the power of this design to these individuals? How might I learn more about these particular students as I watch them interact with the content and the ways in which I set about to teach it? In what ways might I ensure that each learner has full access to the power of this design in accordance with his or her particular needs?

With those questions indelibly in mind, the curriculum plans we make will be energized and informed by awareness of the people for whom they are designed. Curriculum design becomes a process through which we plan to communicate to real human beings our belief in the power of knowledge and the potential of the individual to develop power through knowledge. Appropriately, then, the chapter that follows explores what it means to craft curriculum that empowers learners.

3

WHAT REALLY MATTERS IN LEARNING? (CONTENT)

What knowledge is truly essential and enduring?
What's worth understanding? What powerful ideas should all students encounter?
Can differentiation and standards coexist? How can we address required content standards while remaining responsive to individual students?

Educators from preschool to graduate school typically face a common challenge: too much content to teach given the available time. The problem is magnified in certain fields, such as science and history, where the knowledge base continuously expands. This problem of content "overload" requires teachers to make choices constantly regarding what content to emphasize as well as what not to teach.

In recent years, national subject area associations, states, and provinces in North America have established content standards to specify what students should know and be able to do in the various disciplines during the K–12 school years. These standards are intended to focus teaching and learning, guide curriculum development, and provide a basis for accountability systems. Despite all good intentions and many positive effects, the standards movement has not solved the "overload" problem. In fact, instead of ameliorating the problem, the standards may have exacerbated it.

Consider the findings of researchers Robert Marzano and John Kendall (1998). Their analysis of 160 national and state-level content standards documents yielded a synthesis of 255 standards and 3,968 benchmarks that students are expected to know and do in various subject areas. The researchers went on to calculate that if 30 minutes of instructional time were allocated to each identified benchmark (and many benchmarks require much more time to teach and learn), an additional 15,465 hours (approximately nine more years of school) would be required for students to learn them all! Such ambitious content demands can seem daunting to educators attempting to teach and assess the standards.

In addition to the amount of content identified, standards may be stated in ways that make them difficult to address. Some standards are too big. Consider this one: Students will "recognize how technical, organizational, and aesthetic elements contribute to the ideas, emotions, and overall impact communicated by works of art." Such a statement is simply too global to provide goal clarity and guidance to instruction and assessment. Different teachers in the arts could, in good faith, emphasize very different aspects of the content, while believing that their actions honor the standard.

Conversely, some standards are too small. For example, consider this 7th-grade state history standard that declares that students will "compare the early civilizations of the Indus River Valley in Pakistan with the Huang-He of China." Although this statement provides a much sharper target than the previous example, the focus is too specific and seems somewhat arbitrary. This problem is exacerbated by high-stakes tests that rely on selected-response items to assess the discrete standards and benchmarks. When content is reduced to a series of "factlets" and assessments are built upon decontextualized items, teachers are faced with a laundry list to cover without a sense of priority. The larger, transferable concepts and processes can get lost in a sea of details.

Some states and provinces have attempted to address one or both problems by publishing companion "clarification" documents to explain the intent of the standards, identify more specific grade-level benchmarks, and specify performance indicators. Nonetheless, the challenges of content overload persist.

Content standards are not the only problem; textbooks frequently exacerbate the situation. To meet the requirements of textbook adoption committees looking for congruence with *their* state or provincial standards, commercial textbook companies in the United States and Canada strive to include as many standards and benchmarks as possible. The result is a surfeit of information, a "mile wide, inch deep" treatment of subject area knowledge.

So how can we address the content overload challenges posed by standards and textbooks? In their book *Understanding by Design*, Grant Wiggins and Jay McTighe (2005) propose that learning results should be considered in terms of understanding the "big ideas" and core processes within the content standards. These ideas are framed around provocative "essential questions" to focus teaching and learning. The more specific facts, concepts, and skills (which are typically assessed on standardized tests) are then taught in the context of exploring and applying the larger ideas and processes. This approach is consistent with the recommendations of other experts in curriculum and assessment, such as Lynn Erickson (1998), who calls for "concept-based curriculum," and Douglas Reeves (2002), who advocates framing "power standards" as a means of prioritizing content by focusing on transferable concepts and processes.

So what does this approach look like in practice? Let's revisit the two previous examples.

The first standard in the arts ("recognize how technical, organizational, and aesthetic elements contribute to the ideas, emotions, and overall impact communicated by works of art") is very broad and needs a conceptual focus. Consider the following examples of "big ideas" and companion questions:

• Artists' cultures and personal experiences inspire the ideas and emotions they express. *Where do artists get their ideas? In what ways do culture and experience inspire artistic expression?*

• Available tools and technologies influence the ways in which artists express their ideas. *How does the medium influence the message?*

• Great artists often break with established traditions, conventions, and techniques to express what they see and feel. *What makes art "great"?*

In the second example ("compare the early civilizations of the Indus River Valley in Pakistan with the Huang-He of China"), students would benefit from examining larger ideas and associated questions, such as these:

• The geography, climate, and natural resources of a region influence how its inhabitants live and work. *How does where people live influence how they live?*

• Cultures share common features while retaining unique qualities. *What makes a civilization? Are modern civilizations more "civilized" than ancient ones?*

• The past offers insights into historical patterns, universal themes, and recurring aspects of the human condition. *What can we learn from studying other places and times? How does the past affect us today?*

Notice that in both examples, the transferable "big ideas" and essential questions provide a conceptual lens through which the specific content in the standards may be addressed. More specific facts and skills are then taught in the context of the larger ideas and questions. This approach provides a means of managing large quantities of content knowledge, while supporting meaningful learning. When the curriculum, instruction, and assessment focus on such "big ideas" and essential questions, they signal to students and parents that the underlying goal of all school efforts is to improve student learning of important content, not merely to traverse a textbook or practice for standardized tests.

Planning Backward

If we want students to explore essential questions and come to understand important ideas contained in content standards, then we'll need to plan accordingly. To that end, we propose a three-stage backward design process for curriculum planning.

The concept of planning backward from desired results is not new. In 1949, Ralph Tyler described this approach as an effective process for focusing instruction. More recently, Stephen Covey (1989), in the best-selling book *Seven Habits of Highly Effective People,* reports that effective people in various fields are goal oriented and plan with the end in mind. Although not a new idea, we have found that the deliberate use of backward design for planning courses, units, and individual lessons results in more clearly defined goals, more appropriate assessments, and more purposeful teaching.

Backward planning asks educators to consider the following three stages:

Stage 1. Identify desired results. *What should students know, understand, and be able to do? What content is worthy of understanding? What "enduring" understandings are desired? What essential questions will be explored?* In Stage 1, we consider our goals, examine established content standards (national, state, province, district), and review curriculum expectations. Because there is typically more "content" than can reasonably be addressed within the available time, we are obliged to make choices. This first stage in the design process calls for clarity about priorities.

Stage 2. Determine acceptable evidence. *How will we know whether students have achieved the desired results? What will we accept as evidence of student understanding and proficiency?* Backward design encourages teachers and curriculum planners to "think like an assessor" before designing specific units and lessons. The assessment evidence we need reflects the desired results identified in Stage 1. Thus, we consider *in advance* the assessment evidence needed to document and validate that the targeted learning has been achieved. Doing so sharpens and focuses teaching.

Stage 3. Plan learning experiences and instruction. *What enabling knowledge and skills will students need to perform effectively and achieve desired results? What activities, sequence, and resources are best suited to accomplish our goals?* With clearly identified results and appropriate evidence of understanding in mind, we now think through the most appropriate instructional activities. The goal is to make our teaching engaging *and* effective for learners, while always keeping the end in mind.

We have found that backward design helps avoid two familiar "twin sins" of planning and teaching. The first "sin" occurs more widely at the elementary and middle levels and may be labeled "activity-oriented" instruction. In this case, teacher planning is focused on activities. Often, the activities are engaging, hands-on, and kid-friendly. Those are fine qualities as long as the activities are purposefully focused on clear and important goals *and* if they yield appropriate evidence of learning. In too many cases, however, activity-oriented planning and teaching are like cotton candy—pleasant enough in the moment but lacking long-term substance.

The second "sin," more prevalent at the secondary and collegiate levels, goes by the name of "coverage." In this case, planning means reviewing the teacher's edition and teaching involves a chronological march through the textbook. Indeed, some teachers act as if they believe that their job is to cover the book. In contrast, we believe that a teacher's job is to teach for learning of important content, to check regularly for understanding on the part of all students, and to make needed adjustments based on results. The textbook may very well provide an important resource, but it should *not* constitute the syllabus.

Many teachers have observed that the backward planning process makes sense but feels awkward, as it requires a break from comfortable habits. We have found that when people plan backward, by design, they are much less likely to succumb to the problematic aspects of activity- or coverage-oriented teaching.

A Planning Template

McTighe and Wiggins (2004) have developed a template to assist educators in focusing on important content while planning backward (see Figure 3.1). Figure 3.2 offers a set of planning questions to consider when using the template to plan a unit of study, a course, or a workshop.

Note that in Stage 1, designers are asked to specify desired understandings (Box U) and the companion essential questions (Box Q), reflecting the established learning goals, such as content standards (Box G). These elements help clarify content priorities and ensure that big ideas and important questions are prominent. The more specific knowledge and skill objectives are then listed in Boxes K and S.

Stage 2 distinguishes between two broad types of assessment—performance tasks and other evidence. The performance tasks (Box T) require students to transfer (i.e., to apply) their learning to a new and authentic situation as a means of assessing their understanding. Other evidence, such as a traditional quizzes, tests, observations, and work samples (Box OE) help round out the picture of what students know and can do.

The vertical format of the template facilitates a check for alignment between Stages 1 and 2. One can readily see the extent to which the proposed assessments will provide valid and reliable evidence of the desired learning.

With results and evidence in mind, we now plan purposeful learning activities and directed teaching to help *all* students reach the desired achievements (Box L). It is here, in Stage 3, where the concerns for both content and kids combine in a plan for responsive teaching.

FIGURE 3.1
Planning Template

Stage 1—Desired Results	
Established Goal(s):	**G**
Understanding(s): **U** *Students will understand that . . .*	**Essential Question(s):** **Q**
Students will know . . . **K**	*Students will be able to . . .* **S**

Stage 2—Assessment Evidence	
Performance Task(s): **T**	**Other Evidence:** **OE**

Stage 3—Learning Plan
Learning Activities: **L**

Source: From *Understanding by Design Professional Development Workbook* (p. 31), by J. McTighe and G. Wiggins, 2004, Alexandria, VA: Association for Supervision and Curriculum Development. Copyright 2004 by the Association for Supervision and Curriculum Development. Reprinted with permission.

FIGURE 3.2
Planning Template with Design Questions

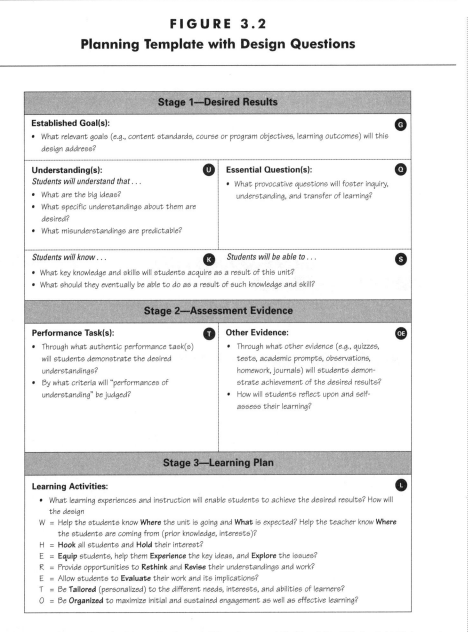

Stage 1—Desired Results

Established Goal(s):   **G**
- What relevant goals (e.g., content standards, course or program objectives, learning outcomes) will this design address?

Understanding(s):   **U** | **Essential Question(s):**   **Q**
Students will understand that . . . |
- What are the big ideas? | - What provocative questions will foster inquiry, understanding, and transfer of learning?
- What specific understandings about them are desired? |
- What misunderstandings are predictable? |

Students will know . . .   **K**   *Students will be able to . . .*   **S**
- What key knowledge and skills will students acquire as a result of this unit?
- What should they eventually be able to do as a result of such knowledge and skill?

Stage 2—Assessment Evidence

Performance Task(s):   **T** | **Other Evidence:**   **OE**
- Through what authentic performance task(s) will students demonstrate the desired understandings? | - Through what other evidence (e.g., quizzes, tests, academic prompts, observations, homework, journals) will students demonstrate achievement of the desired results?
- By what criteria will "performances of understanding" be judged? | - How will students reflect upon and self-assess their learning?

Stage 3—Learning Plan

Learning Activities: **L**
- What learning experiences and instruction will enable students to achieve the desired results? How will the design
- W = Help the students know **Where** the unit is going and **What** is expected? Help the teacher know **Where** the students are coming from (prior knowledge, interests)?
- H = **Hook** all students and **Hold** their interest?
- E = **Equip** students, help them **Experience** the key ideas, and **Explore** the issues?
- R = Provide opportunities to **Rethink** and **Revise** their understandings and work?
- E = Allow students to **Evaluate** their work and its implications?
- T = Be **Tailored** (personalized) to the different needs, interests, and abilities of learners?
- O = Be **Organized** to maximize initial and sustained engagement as well as effective learning?

Source: From *Understanding by Design Professional Development Workbook* (p. 30), by J. McTighe and G. Wiggins, 2004, Alexandria, VA: Association for Supervision and Curriculum Development. Copyright 2004 by the Association for Supervision and Curriculum Development. Reprinted with permission.

Frequently Asked Questions About Backward Design

Predictable questions arise as teachers begin to use backward design for planning. We'll address three of the most frequent questions here.

How do we identify the "big ideas" that we want students to understand? How do we develop the accompanying essential questions?

We suggest using national, state, or provincial content standards as a starting point. Often, the standards themselves, or companion clarification documents, present important ideas contained within. A more specific strategy involves "unpacking" the nouns and verbs in the standards. The nouns point to "big ideas" and companion questions, whereas the verbs are suggestive of the assessments. Because one needs a solid base of content knowledge to identify the enduring ideas and essential questions, we recommend planning with a partner or team whenever possible. In this case, two (or three) heads are almost always better.

Another process involves interrogating the content using questions such as these: Why exactly are we teaching _____? What do we want students to understand and be able to do five years from now? If this unit is a story, what's the moral? What couldn't people do if they didn't understand _____?

Finally, we encourage people to "work smarter" by consulting resources such as the UbD Exchange Web site (http://ubdexchange.org), which contains thousands of examples of unit designs in UbD format, as well as numerous Web links for finding "big ideas," essential questions, performance assessment tasks, and rubrics. It makes no sense to reinvent the wheel.

Do you have to follow the template order (top to bottom) when you design?

No. Backward design does not demand a rigid sequence. Although there is a clear logic to the template, the planning process typically unfolds in an iterative, back-and-forth fashion. The template is important not as a series of boxes in a prescribed order but as a tool for developing a coherent, purposeful, and efficient design for learning. Many teachers report that once they become familiar with backward design through using the physical template, they develop a "mental template"—a way of thinking and planning. Like any effective graphic organizer or process tool, the template leaves a cognitive residue that enhances curriculum planning.

Can you use the three stages of backward design to plan a lesson as well as a unit?

We recommend the unit as a focus for backward design because the key elements of the template—big idea understandings, essential questions, and performance assessments—are complex and require more time than is available within a single lesson. However, we have found that when lessons (Stage 3) are planned under an umbrella of desired results (Stage 1) and appropriate assessments (Stage 2), more purposeful teaching and improved learning follow.

Standards and Responsive Teaching: Planning for Content *and* Kids

In the previous section, we proposed a three-stage "backward design" process for planning units and courses. Now, we'll examine that process more closely with differentiation in mind.

In Stage 1 of backward design, we identify desired results, including relevant content standards. If appropriately selected, these established goals (placed in Box G of the template) serve as a focal point for teaching *all* students. The "big ideas" that we want students to come to understand (Box U) and their companion essential questions (Box Q) provide intellectual richness and promote transfer of learning. Like the content standards, desired understandings and questions should remain a constant target, regardless of differences in students' background knowledge, interests, and preferred learning modalities. In other words, the big ideas and essential questions provide the conceptual pillars that anchor the various disciplines. We do not arbitrarily amend these based on *whom* we are teaching.[1] Of course, the nature and needs of learners should certainly influence *how* we teach toward these targets.

The more specific knowledge and skill objectives (Boxes K and S) are linked to the desired standards and understandings, yet some differentiation may well be needed here. Because students typically vary in their prior knowledge and skill levels, responsive teachers target their instruction to address significant gaps in knowledge and skills. Such responsiveness follows from effective diagnostic assessments that reveal if such prerequisite knowledge and skills exist. There is a place for sensitivity to student needs in Stage

1 without compromising the established standards or the integrity of subject areas.

The logic of backward design dictates that evidence derives from goals. Thus, in Stage 2, teachers are asked to "think like assessors" to determine the assessments that will provide the evidence for the identified knowledge, skills, and understandings in Stage 1. To this end, we have found it fruitful to examine the verbs in the content standard and benchmark statements because these suggest the nature of the needed evidence. A standard that uses verbs such as "know" or "identify" implies that an objective test could provide an appropriate measure. For example, a standard that calls for students to "know the capitals of states (or provinces)" could be assessed through a matching or multiple-choice test format.

However, a standard that expects students to "apply," "analyze," or "explain"—to thoughtfully use their knowledge and skill—demands different methods for verifying achievement. For example, if the standard states, "students analyze factors that influence location of capital cities," then an appropriate assessment would expect an explanation of the influence of various geographic, economic, and political factors.

Along these lines, when we consider the big ideas we want students to "understand," we need to concurrently consider the evidence that will show that students truly understand them. In this regard, Wiggins and McTighe (1998) propose that understanding is best revealed through various facets— when learners can *explain, interpret, apply, shift perspective, display empathy,* and *reflectively self-assess.* In other words, we need to match our assessment measures with our goals.

While the needed evidence, in general, is determined by the desired results, the *particulars* of an assessment can, nonetheless, be tailored to accommodate the uniqueness of students. Consider a science standard that calls for a basic understanding of "life cycles." Evidence of this understanding could be obtained by having students explain the concept and offer an illustrative example. Such evidence could be collected in writing, but such a requirement would be inappropriate for an English language learner whose skills in written English are limited. Indeed, her difficulty expressing herself in writing could yield the incorrect inference that she does not understand life cycles. However, if she is offered flexibility in the response mode, such as explaining orally or visually, we will obtain a more valid measure of her understanding.

It is important to note that although we may offer students options to show what they know and can do, we will use the *same* criteria in judging the response. In the previous example, a student's explanation of life cycles must be accurate, thorough, and include an appropriate illustrative example, *regardless* of whether the student responded orally, visually, or in writing. In other words, the criteria are derived primarily from the content goal, not the response mode. If we vary the criteria for different students, then we can no longer claim that our tests are standards based and criterion referenced.

Of course, feasibility must be considered. Teachers will need to find the practical balance point between completely individualized assessments and standardized, "one-size-fits-all" measures. Nonetheless, we believe that classroom assessments can indeed be responsive to students' differences while still providing reliable information about student learning.

Finally, we come to Stage 3, where we develop our teaching and learning plan to help students achieve the desired results of Stage 1 and equip them for their "performances of understanding" in Stage 2. In Stage 3, responsive teaching flourishes as we consider variety in the background knowledge, interests, and preferred learning modalities of our students. A variety of specific approaches and techniques for responsive teaching will be discussed in later chapters.

We conclude this chapter by offering a visual summary of the preceding narrative—one way of representing the relationship between backward design and differentiation—in Figure 3.3. It supports the premise that enduring understandings, essential knowledge, and essential skills should be a steady focus for the vast majority of learners, that *how* students demonstrate proficiency can be responsive to student readiness, interest, and/or mode of learning, and that the steps leading students toward proficiency with the essentials should be differentiated in ways that maximize the growth of individual learners in regard to the essential learning goals.

A river needs banks to flow. Backward design provides the structure to support flexibility in teaching and assessing in order to honor the integrity of content while respecting the individuality of learners. The blending of UbD and DI provides stability of focus on essential knowledge, understanding,

FIGURE 3.3
Applying Differentiation to the UbD Framework

This organizer provides a general framework for thinking about where differentiation may apply in the Understanding by Design framework. There will be exceptions to the general rule of adhering to the same essential knowledge, understanding, and skill in the case of students who have extreme needs. For example, a student with an Individualized Education Program (IEP) or a student who is very new to the English language may need work with skills that are precursors to the ones specified in the framework. Similarly, an advanced learner who demonstrates proficiency with the essential knowledge and skill specified in the framework needs to work with more advanced knowledge and skill in order to continue developing as a learner. In regard to Assessment Evidence, although content goals assessed will remain constant for most learners, varying the mode of assessment will benefit many learners.

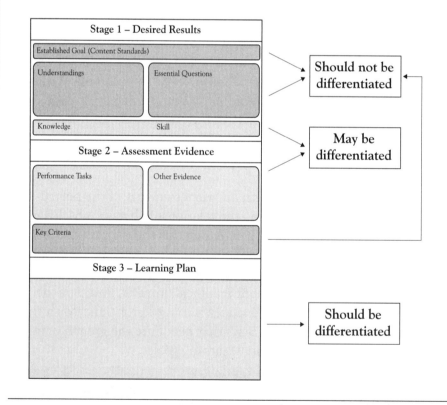

and skill and flexibility in guiding learners to the desired ends. The chapter that follows explores ways in which differentiation flows from and is shaped by quality curriculum.

Note

1. In cases where Individualized Education Programs (IEPs) have been developed for exceptional students, then the particular goals of their plan are added to, or substituted for, the content standards as indicated by the IEP.

4

WHAT REALLY MATTERS IN PLANNING FOR STUDENT SUCCESS?

What are the attitudes and skills of responsive teachers, and why do they matter?
What might the attitudes and skills of successful planning for differentiation look like in practice?
What are indicators of effective differentiation in the classroom?

Compelling Curriculum—and the Other Half of the Teaching Equation

It is vital to be clear about what is essential in content. Certainly such clarity reflects an understanding of what experts have identified as the core of those disciplines. Such clarity also indicates our awareness that learning has much more to do with one's ability to organize and use ideas and skills to address problems than with retention of data. In addition, clarity about content reveals our awareness that human beings seek to make sense of their world and that the big ideas of the disciplines reveal the big ideas of life. Inevitably, to grasp the key concepts and principles of any subject also helps us better understand ourselves, our lives, and our world.

Clarity about what really matters in the disciplines enables us to teach for understanding. To teach for understanding is to provide the sort of intellectual diet that yields thoughtful, capable, confident learners—and citizens. Said another way, the more powerful the curriculum, the greater the possibilities for the classroom, the teacher, and the students.

Even in the presence of high-quality curriculum, however, the job of the teacher is far from complete. If we see ourselves predominantly as teachers of curriculum—even exemplary curriculum—we have forgotten half of our professional role. We are also teachers of human beings. The essence of our job is making sure that the curriculum serves as a catalyst for powerful learning for students who, with our guidance and support, become skilled in and committed to the process of learning.

In other words, to be effective, teachers must continually attend to the quality of both curriculum and instruction. Attending to quality of curriculum while de-emphasizing instruction may provide great mental stimulation for teachers but is unlikely to do the same for the young people we serve. On the other hand, attention to quality of instruction without an equal emphasis on curriculum may provide novelty or entertainment for students, but it will almost certainly *not* result in durable and potent learning outcomes.

Because the human beings we teach differ significantly in many dimensions, the means by which we attempt to make a rich curriculum "work" for those students will have to be many and varied. A key premise of differentiation is that virtually all students[1] should have access to a curriculum rich with the ideas and skills valued by experts in a field. That is both a lofty and a necessary ideal. We translate it into reality when we say to ourselves, "There are many ways I can help my students learn. My job is to find enough ways to teach and enough ways to support learning so that what I teach works for each person who needs to learn the essential content."

Essential Attitudes and Skills of Differentiated Instruction

Research suggests that most teachers believe it is desirable to attend to learner variance as they teach. This is the case across grades and subjects and among teachers of all experiential levels. Research also suggests to us that few teachers in fact translate that ideal into classroom practice.

At least a part of the reason so many of us fall short of implementing the kind of responsive classrooms we believe would help students succeed is that we have few models of how such classrooms would look and little personal experience with the concept. The result is that we don't really know how to get from Point A, where many of us practice right now, to Point B, where many of us would like our practice to be.

A worthy step in that direction is looking at key attitudes and skills necessary for differentiated or responsive teaching. With those elements in front of us, we are at least better equipped to measure our own particular instructional strengths and needs and to set a course for persistent movement toward the kinds of classrooms that fully support the success of academically diverse student populations.

At least nine attitudes and skills typify teachers who help all learners:

- They establish clarity about curricular essentials.
- They accept responsibility for learner success.
- They develop communities of respect.
- They build awareness of what works for each student.
- They develop classroom management routines that contribute to success.
- They help students become effective partners in their own success.
- They develop flexible classroom teaching routines.
- They expand a repertoire of instructional strategies.
- They reflect on individual progress with an eye toward curricular goals and personal growth.

The stronger we are as professionals in each of these areas, the more successful our students are likely to be as learners. Significant deficits in any of the areas are likely to result in learning deficits for at least some of the students who count on us. Following is a brief examination of the meaning of each of the attitudes and skills, an explanation of why the attitude or skill is significant in student success, and how it might look in practice.

Establishing Clarity About Curricular Essentials

In various places throughout this book, we have made the case that curriculum should focus on the knowledge, understanding, and skill that enables students to develop solid frameworks of meaning in a topic or discipline. That goal matters because as teachers we progress toward expertise in our profession as we continually refine our own understanding of what in a topic or subject is genuinely significant. The goal matters because we can't teach everything (and, more to the point, students can't learn everything), and we ought to take care to teach that which is most durable and useful. It matters because teaching what is authentically central to a topic or discipline serves as a "representation" of the topic or field and helps young people think more effectively about the broader topic or discipline when they are called upon to do so beyond our classroom. In other words, the case for curriculum that is focused on what is enduring in content stands on its own merits. Nonetheless, clarity about curricular essentials is also critical for differentiated or responsive teaching for yet another reason.

Curricular goals are the springboard from which differentiation ought to begin. If, as a teacher, I am foggy about precisely what students should know, understand, and be able to do as the result of a unit or lesson, I may differentiate instruction, but I am likely to generate multiple versions of fog. Furthermore, if I am uncertain of the precise outcomes for a unit (and thus for how a particular lesson or product serves those outcomes), I am also unable to preassess students' proximity to those outcomes effectively—and thus I am not certain how to craft the start of the learning journey for students whose proficiencies vary.

It is the case in many classrooms now that teachers attempt to "differentiate" instruction by giving struggling learners less to do than other students and by giving more advanced students more to do than other learners. It is not helpful to struggling students to do less of what they do not grasp. Nor is it helpful to advanced students to do more of what they already understood before they began the task. It is likely that the "more" or "less" approach to differentiation occurs when we lack clarity about essential outcomes and thus a meaningful basis from which to differentiate.

In an effectively differentiated classroom, the same powerful understanding-based goals will nearly always "belong" to everyone. A teacher will begin by preassessing learners' proficiency with those goals. With that information in hand, the teacher can assist some students in developing precursor proficiencies necessary for continued growth and other students in extending their competencies related to the goals. Moreover, the teacher has a road map for the learning journey that directs ongoing assessment and adjustment of teaching and learning plans throughout the unit— just as it directs construction of the unit.

Teacher clarity related to understanding-based teaching and learning goals has other compelling implications for differentiation:

• When learning outcomes are powerful and belong to everyone in the class, the teacher is able to communicate to the students the importance of the classroom agenda and the capacity of every student to benefit from and contribute to that agenda. This is an important factor in creating a learning environment that is affirming to each student in the classroom.

• Curriculum based on the important concepts and principles of the disciplines is more likely to be engaging to students and link their particular life experiences and interests with the curriculum. This is important in establishing relevance for varied learners, leading to enhanced motivation to learn.

• Curriculum based on enduring understandings is more flexible in its "entry points" for students than is a largely fact-based, linear curriculum of coverage. That is, there is a kindergarten version and a Ph.D. version of the big ideas of the disciplines. An opportunity thus always exists for students with varied backgrounds, strengths, deficits, and developmental stages to work with the essential ideas at levels of complexity appropriate for their current needs. This approach helps us avoid the pitfall of assuming that students who struggle with school should focus largely on drills of information as a precursor to powerful learning—thus differentiating for struggling learners by lowering expectations. It also helps us avoid the pitfall of differentiating for advanced learners by giving them something "entertaining," rather than extending their level of expertise with essential ideas and skills. Thus rich curriculum is critical in addressing student readiness while ensuring that all students construct an enduring framework for understanding a discipline.

• When a teacher is clear about the enduring understandings of a lesson or unit, that teacher is more likely to be at ease in offering students options to explore and express learning in a mode appropriate for the student's learning profile. The teacher does not "give up" anything in allowing a student to work alone or with a partner, or to express an idea in a more divergent versus convergent format. It is the outcome that matters, and whatever route to the outcome works for a student is likely to be a help rather than a hindrance in constructing student success. It is important in addressing the wide learning profile variance represented in most contemporary classrooms. Therefore, although understanding-based curriculum exemplifies best practice in designing *what* students will learn, it is also essential to designing *how* they will learn.

Scenario

Ms. Kanefsky and her 3rd graders are studying the westward movement of populations during the time when the United States began to expand rapidly beyond the East Coast. Two of the enduring understandings of the unit are that change involves risk and that change can be both positive and negative.

On the unit pre-assessment, Ms. Kanefsky gathered information about essential knowledge (such as vocabulary) and essential skills (such as map reading) that students would encounter during the unit. She also asked them to write or draw about (1) a change in their lives or in the life of a family member that involved a move or taking a risk and (2) an example from history when change had been positive and when it had been negative. This portion of the assessment helped her develop an early sense of the degree to which each learner could relate to the unit's enduring understandings. The teacher did not grade the pre-assessment but rather used the data to determine who might need particular assistance with essential skills and knowledge. She also used the students' own stories as a way to begin connecting classroom discussions about westward migration with the students' experiences. Furthermore, she was able to see who could readily apply the principles to earlier work in social studies and who had difficulty in doing so. The pre-assessment data helped her make initial, informed decisions about particular assignments and early student groupings in the unit.

One aspect of the unit involved all students in the class making a simulated journey west. Each student kept records of the journey and reflected on events (with teacher guidance) along the way. Students who were more concrete in their thinking about the unit's enduring understandings wrote a series of letters to a person "back home," in which they—among other things—talked about risks they experienced and the positives and negatives of change. Students more readily able to work with abstractions related to the unit's enduring understandings wrote a reflective diary examining both the events and their thoughts about the events as they related to the unit's identified understandings. Also in the class were several students with IEPs for mild retardation. The teacher worked with these students to create a trip quilt that reflected risk and the positives and negatives of change in visual images. She also integrated IEP vocabulary into the assignment for the students so they could develop required skills in a shared context of meaning.

Students frequently shared their work with students from other groups and with the whole class as a way of extending their learning by drawing on the work of peers.

Accepting Responsibility for Learner Success

Certainly most of us understand that the role of the teacher is central in student success. Nonetheless, it is easy to develop habits that lure us away from the reality that we are better teachers when we accept responsibility for the success of each student. We try to develop "good lessons," and we try to "deliver them well." We begin to live at peace with an "I taught it well so they should have gotten it" approach to our work. It's a very different teacher who accepts the reality that if a student has not yet learned a thing of importance, the teacher has not yet taught it well enough. If a student is not growing—even if he or she is making As—the teacher is not teaching that student.

In an effectively differentiated classroom, a teacher adheres to a philosophy that each learner is sent to school by someone who has to trust that the teacher will realize the worth of the child and be guided by a sense of stewardship of potential each time the child enters the classroom door. In other words, the teacher accepts the premise that if he or she doesn't ensure that the day works for the child, it may be a lost day.

Clearly, the students also have responsibilities regarding learning. In fact, part of the teacher's job is to establish an environment in which shared responsibility for successful learning is part of the classroom ethic and practice. Certainly students are better off when parents play active roles in their children's learning. Obviously it is better when a student comes to school with positive motivation and behavior. Nonetheless, a teacher in an effectively differentiated classroom will not allow economics, gender, race, past achievement, lack of parental involvement, or any other factor to become an excuse for shoddy work or outcomes that are less than a student is able to accomplish.

In such classrooms, the teacher believes he or she must

• Get to know each student as a means of teaching him or her effectively.

• Continually map the progress of students against essential outcomes.

• Find alternate ways of teaching and alternate paths to learning to ensure continual growth of each student.

• Send consistent messages to students that if something didn't work today, both teacher and student will be back at it tomorrow and the day after until success occurs.

• Provide support systems that persistently articulate to students and model for them what quality work looks like and what it takes to attain quality results.

Scenario

Four students in Mrs. Pasarella's class lack past math skills necessary to become confident with current operations. Three students already demonstrate mastery of outcomes specified for the end of the unit. The teacher finds several times in the week to work intensely with the struggling students to help them become proficient with precursor understandings and skills. She also uses some alternate homework assignments for these students so they have the opportunity to "patch the holes" in their mathematical understanding. At the same time, she works closely with them to ensure that they are developing foundational understanding of the newly introduced concepts, understandings, and skills so that they do not continue to fall further behind. The teacher also meets with the students who are advanced. They are completing a longer-term assignment that calls on them to combine various facets of mathematical understanding and even to "invent" new ideas to solve a complex, multistep problem. At any point in the unit when these students demonstrate competence with outcomes, the long-term assignment replaces assignments that would require them to rehearse what they already know, and it calls on them to extend their reach mathematically rather than waiting or "marching in place."

Developing Communities of Respect

Classrooms are small universes. In those universes, we learn to accept and appreciate one another's variances—or we learn to resent and be suspicious of differences. We learn to celebrate one another's victories and support one another's efforts—or we learn to compete in ways that undermine rather than dignify those with whom we share time and space.

In a differentiated classroom, it is crucial for students to accept and ultimately understand both their commonalities and differences. The classroom has to be a place where each student feels safe (not seen as a failure, a nerd, a test score, a social pariah) and also challenged (to become the best it is in that student to be). An atmosphere of unequivocal respect for each member of the learning community opens doors of possibility for each member of that community. It is not necessary in a differentiated classroom that everyone become best friends, but it is vitally important to treat one another with respect.

Teachers in such classrooms

• Attend to each student in ways that communicate respect and positive expectation.

• Seek out, affirm, and draw on the unique abilities of each learner.

• Elicit and value multiple perspectives on issues, decisions, and ways of accomplishing the work of the class.

• Make sure all students are called upon to participate regularly—with no student or group of students either dominating the class or receding from participation in it.

• Help students identify and adhere to constructive ways of interacting with one another.

• Design tasks that enable each student to make important contributions to the work of the group.

• Ensure that the languages, cultures, and perspectives of varied cultures are represented in the important work of the group.

• Help students reflect on the quality of their contributions to the developing classroom community.

• Seek and respond to students' ideas about how to foster respect in the classroom.

Scenario

Mr. Alvarez has cultivated several habits that serve him well. He invites parents of all of his students to important classroom presentations, ensuring that parents know their student will be spotlighted while they are present. He keeps a quick tally of students he calls on so that he makes certain he communicates the expectation that everyone will contribute to the class. He regularly includes the contributions of people from many ethnic and language groups to the field he and his students study. He frequently constructs class-room groups of students whose interests and strengths differ; the task that he presents to the group will thus draw on the abilities of each student. He makes it a point to study the cultures of his students so that his understanding of their experiences continually deepens.

Building Awareness of What Works for Each Student

Teachers in effectively differentiated classrooms are hunters and gatherers of information about what best propels learning for each student. Such teachers believe that each new piece of information contributes to accruing insight about how to work more effectively with a given learner.

Teachers in such classrooms

• Make opportunities to communicate individually with individual learners.

• Garner information on students' interests, dreams, and aspirations.

• Work to understand each student's profile of academic strengths and weaknesses.

• Seek to understand the inevitable learning profile variance that exists in groups and individuals.

• Observe students working individually, in small groups, and in the class as a whole with the intent to study factors that facilitate or impede progress for individuals and for the group as a whole.

• Create opportunities to learn from parents, guardians, and community members about students.

Scenario

Mrs. Callison keeps notes on her students throughout the year. She has a notebook with a page for each student she teaches, in alphabetical order by class. Sometimes when students are working alone or in small groups, she walks among them, observes what they are doing, and jots interesting observations on sticky notes. At the end of the day, she puts the dated notes on the appropriate student pages. She also uses the pages to record pertinent insights from parents, things students say to her that she wants to remember, and results from formal interest and learning profile surveys she gives students at key points in the year. She is always amazed how much information the notebook contains, even by the end of the first marking period. She is also continually surprised by how much of the information she would forget if it were not written down.

Developing Classroom Management Routines That Contribute to Success

Handling all the components of a daily classroom routine is difficult—even in a classroom where the group nearly always works as a single unit. Directions need to be written on the board. Materials have to be secured, distributed, and collected. Student work needs to be checked in or filed. And all the while, someone needs help with something. The multiplicity of tasks in the classroom combined with their frequency and rotation is one reason why teaching is so exhausting.

Even in a classroom where the expectation is that everyone will work on the same task within the same time frame, it is difficult for the teacher to do all that needs doing. And always, there is the concern about whether students are sitting still, listening, behaving. In the early part of a teacher's career, success almost becomes defined by the ability to return papers without having student behavior explode.

In a differentiated classroom, there is not even the expectation that everyone will complete the same task, using the same materials, and under the same time constraints. It is, in fact, no longer possible to manage the classroom with "frontal control." Thus developing a system through which students learn to play a large role in managing themselves, their work, and their success is not an ideal but a necessity.

In truth, it is neither necessary nor wise for a teacher in any setting to do all that needs doing in a classroom. Not only are students capable of doing many of the routine operations in a classroom, but they benefit from the responsibility. They become more aware of classroom operations, more independent as thinkers and problem solvers, more a part of a team effort, and they develop more ownership in outcomes. In addition, the teacher is then free to provide the kind of assistance to students that makes good use of his or her professional abilities. Differentiated classrooms enlist everyone's best efforts in making sure the classroom operates smoothly.

Teachers in such classrooms

• Have a clear image of what the classroom should look like when it functions smoothly.

• Establish high expectations for the smooth operation of classroom routines as an important factor in student growth.

• Study operational routines to make sure they are working well for individuals, the class, and the teachers.

• Work with students to develop a rationale and rules for effective classroom operation.

• Make clear on an ongoing basis criteria for success in varied roles and in varied tasks.

• Gather information from students about what is and is not working well for them as individuals and as part of small groups.

• Seek student advice on making the class operate effectively.

• Enlist students in performing routine functions whenever possible.

• Help students perform those functions effectively and efficiently.

• Ensure everyone's participation in making the classroom work.

Scenario

Mr. Connelly begins a conversation with his students during the first week of school about what sort of classroom rules and routines they would need in order to help every student succeed beyond his or her expectations. The goal of student success is the ongoing benchmark for establishing and evaluating classroom procedures for the rest of the year. Students make suggestions for how various classroom routines should work. Mr. Connelly formalizes the procedures, reviews them with students prior to implementing them, and asks students to reflect with him on how the procedures worked to help them work effectively and efficiently. He also shares his perspectives with them. They continue to refine routines together throughout the year. He often notes to the students and his colleagues that over the years, his students have taught him a great deal about effective classroom leadership.

Helping Students Become Effective Partners in Their Own Success

Not only is it important in a differentiated classroom for students to be the teacher's partners in operating the classroom effectively, but it is also critical for them to develop increasing awareness of their own learning goals and needs, and to become effective in speaking about and playing a role in addressing those needs. Once again, there is both a more generic reason to help students become effective in charting their own success and reasons more specific to a differentiated classroom.

Surely a part of one's education is developing a growing sophistication about one's strengths and weaknesses, understanding what facilitates and hinders one's learning, setting and monitoring personal learning goals, and so on. To fail in helping students become independent in these ways is to fail in helping them become the sort of perennial learner they need to be to succeed in an increasingly complex world. It is really to fail in helping them become more fully human.

In a differentiated classroom, helping students become increasingly more self-reliant in learning is also propelled by the need to provide differently for different learners in order to maximize their growth. The teacher, then, cannot assume that everyone always needs to read the same book, answer the same question, or receive the same kind of help. In a classroom composed of many individuals, it becomes increasingly important for those individuals to participate in crafting their own success. They need to be able to say that particular work is too hard or too easy for them. They need to be able to distinguish between more productive and less productive working arrangements. They need to be able to determine when they are moving toward goals and when they are becoming derailed. They need to be able to set personal goals beyond those established for the class as a whole. When students develop those sorts of abilities, the teacher's potential for success expands, as does that of the student.

Teachers in such classrooms will do the following:

• Help students understand, accept, and ultimately benefit from their differences.
• Nurture a growing awareness of students' particular strengths.
• Explain the benefit in extending students' strengths.
• Help students acknowledge areas of weakness.
• Facilitate ways to remediate or compensate for weaknesses.
• Guide students in developing a vocabulary related to learning preferences and in exercising those preferences that facilitate their growth.
• Ask students to reflect on their own growth, factors that facilitate that growth, and likely next steps to ensure continual growth.
• Support students in setting and monitoring personal learning goals.

- Provide opportunities for students to talk with their parents or guardians about their growth and goals.

Scenario

Ms. Jacoby establishes some learning goals for the class as a whole. These typically stem from state and local requirements for students in her grade level and subject. From the beginning of the year, however, she talks with students about the need to set personal goals. Sometimes the goals enable students to push forward their talents and interests. Sometimes they cause students to work with areas that are troublesome to them. Early in the year, she provides sample language for goal setting. As the year progresses, students become more comfortable in developing goals without using teacher or peer models. Whenever she can, Ms. Jacoby also has individual conferences with students, asking them to analyze with her a particular piece of work and guiding them in setting goals based on those conversations. Students in her class routinely use rubrics with teacher-generated elements and indicators as well as elements and indicators they establish for themselves.

Developing Flexible Classroom Teaching Routines

Perhaps the defining question in a differentiated classroom is, What's one more way I can think about this? Because the basic premise of differentiated classrooms is that different individuals learn differently, teachers whose practice reflects a philosophy of responsive teaching continually seek varied ways of thinking about time, materials, tasks, student groupings, teacher-guided instruction, space, grading, and so on. Simply put, there is no other way to craft a classroom that works well for each learner.

Teachers in such classrooms will take the following actions:

- Allow for students' different paces of learning.
- Gather both basic and supplementary materials of different readability levels that reflect different cultures, connect with varied interests, and are in different modes (e.g., auditory and visual).
- Experiment with ways to rearrange furniture to allow for whole-class, small-group, and individual learning spaces.
- Vary student groupings so that in addition to meeting readiness needs, they enable students to work with peers who have similar and dissimilar

interests, similar and dissimilar learning preferences, in random groups, in groups selected by the teacher, and in those students select themselves.

• Regularly teach to the whole class, to small groups based on assessed need, and to individuals.

• Teach in a variety of ways to accommodate students' varied readiness needs, interests, and learning preferences.

• Ensure that grades communicate both personal growth and relative standing in regard to specified learning outcomes.

Scenario

Mr. LeMay was comfortable for many years when he lectured to his high school students. His lectures tended to present information in a logical way with the assumption that students would follow his line of thought and draw conclusions about the importance of the topics and issues on which he presented. Over time, he has discovered that more students remain engaged in class when he combines demonstration, storytelling, and visual images with his lectures. He now provides graphic organizers for students who find them helpful in charting key ideas and supporting illustrations. He pauses more often to engage students in discussion about critical understandings. It has been particularly helpful to many students that he now points out essential ideas that the lecture will illustrate as he begins a class. For these students, seeing the big picture before the details contributes greatly to their understanding.

Expanding a Repertoire of Instructional Strategies

A classroom in which one or two instructional strategies predominate is something like a dining room that serves only one or two items. Even if the items are well prepared, they become monotonous to those who must consume them every day.

When a teacher comfortably and appropriately uses an array of instructional strategies, tasks become more engaging to learners. An element of variety, novelty, and surprise is injected into the classroom. Furthermore, some strategies are likely to be more effective in achieving a particular learning goal than would others, and the teacher who has many instructional tools at hand is better equipped to find the tool that fits the purpose.

In regard to differentiation, instructional strategies take on additional significance. Having access to a variety of approaches to teaching and learning gives teachers agility in reaching out to students. It will nearly always be the case that some students prefer certain instructional approaches over others. The teacher who regularly employs a range of strategies is more likely to connect what needs to be learned with the full range of students who need to learn it. In addition, through careful observation of students as they work in a range of instructional settings, a teacher can continue to develop insights about approaches that are most successful for particular learners, as well as for the class as a whole.

Teachers in such classrooms

• Use a variety of strategies when they present to the class as well as when students are actively engaged in learning.

• Use strategies that enable them to address readiness, interest, and learning profile needs.

• Guide students in understanding how to work with instructional approaches effectively.

• Help students reflect on which strategies work well for them, why that might be the case, and what that reveals to the student about him- or herself as a learner.

Scenario

Mr. Castelanos teaches secondary science. He regularly uses a number of strategies designed to support students' development of reading and writing. As he introduces new chapters in the text to the class, he guides students in surveying the chapter for what he calls "landmarks"—the chapter's organization, boldfaced items, important charts, interesting photographs, and so on. He asks the students to read with a particular purpose in mind and often has them assist in setting the purpose as they complete the chapter overview. Follow-up discussions focus not only on important ideas from the text but also on how students used the text to help establish those understandings. He uses think-alouds to model thoughtful reading of complex passages for his students. He regularly provides his students with graphic organizers that they can elect to use as he lectures and when they read text, supplementary, and Internet materials. Furthermore, he ensures that in each presentation he makes to the class, he uses at least two or three modes of presentation—for example, modeling, speaking, graphic representation of ideas, or print. He also makes certain that he reminds students of the "big picture" meaning of what they are studying as well as providing details about the topics. In addition, he regularly uses small-group instruction to enable him to address specific and changing needs of clusters of students in his class.

When students are working on tasks, he often gives them the choice of working alone or collaboratively. As the year progresses, he introduces students to four student-centered instructional approaches that seem to work well for his age group and subject while also addressing the mix of learning needs in his class. He uses learning contracts and tiered assignments to enable students to work at their readiness levels. He uses collaborative controversy with mixed-readiness groups to help students explore important issues in the discipline. He also uses a multiple intelligence approach to encourage students to express what they are learning in ways that are interesting and effective for them.

Reflecting on Individual Progress with an Eye Toward Curricular Goals and Personal Growth

Classrooms are dynamic rather than static. Yesterday's sticking point for three students will become tomorrow's victory. Even student interests and approaches to learning will evolve as time and contexts change.

In an effectively differentiated classroom, curricular essentials provide a sort of anchor in a sea of perpetual change. It is not the expectation of the teacher that all students will arrive in the classroom with the same skills, dispositions, or needs. In fact, the teacher is prepared to address learning gaps as well as needs for accelerated learning.

Nonetheless, the knowledge, understanding, and skill specified as essential for each unit benchmarks student progress. The teacher persistently charts individual standing in regard to those in-common essentials. At the same time, however, the teacher tracks the growth of individuals relative to their own particular profiles. A student whose learning challenges make it difficult to demonstrate full mastery of grade-level skills, for example, should still show noteworthy growth from his starting point. A student who came to the classroom with advanced mastery of key skills should likewise show growth beyond those requirements.

In every subject, a sort of trajectory of learning begins when school starts and continues well beyond the final hour of high school. A teacher in a differentiated classroom understands and deals with both the segment of the trajectory assigned to the particular grade level posted on the student's schedule, and the range of segments represented in the real lives of the human beings in the classroom.

Teachers in such classrooms

• Use pre-assessment data to begin planning for both in-common learning goals and individual learning needs.

• Use ongoing assessment to ensure as close a match as possible between instruction and learner needs.

• Keep track of student growth relative to in-common goals.

• Observe personal growth relative to a student's particular profile.

• Engage students in setting personal goals and evaluating progress toward those goals.

• Reflect consistently on individual and group growth in order to adjust instruction in ways of greatest benefit to individuals and the class as a whole.

• Help parents understand a student's personal growth and standing relative to in-common goals.

Scenario

Through pre-assessment and ongoing observation of student work, Ms. Lampas is aware of a wide range of writing proficiencies in her class. Some students write with ease well beyond grade-level expectations. Other students struggle mightily to record even simple ideas on paper. All students are working right now with main idea development in their writing. Students need to be able to select an issue, develop a plan for writing about what is important related to the issue, and provide both reasons and details about those reasons in order to justify and support their viewpoint on the issue. The class as a whole explores the goals and guidelines for their work.

To support students who have great difficulty with writing, Ms. Lampas meets with them in small groups to brainstorm for issues, map out what is important in an issue, develop a position, chart reasons for their beliefs, and give details about their thinking. Students who meet in these small-group sessions can use the group-generated plan as the basis for their own writing or develop their own issue, plan, reasons, and details.

She also meets in a small group with advanced writers. In this setting, she challenges them to develop multiple viewpoints on the issues they select, to work for the most compelling reasons possible for their positions, and to use details and vocabulary that have the greatest power to illustrate their ideas.

All students have the opportunity to try out their ideas on peers as they write and edit. Ms. Lampas is also available to give in-process feedback and to coach individuals. She notes students' competencies on a checklist that delineates key writing competencies over a multigrade span. This approach allows her to spot the needs of particular students, assess the standing of each student in regard to grade-level benchmarks, and recognize growth from a student's starting point.

The Common Sense of It All

There's no such thing as the perfect lesson, the perfect day in school, or the perfect teacher. For teachers and students alike, the goal is not perfection but persistence in the pursuit of understanding important things.

Differentiated or responsive teaching really stems from an affirmative answer to three questions—and dogged determination to live out the answer in our classrooms a little bit better today than we did yesterday.

1. Do we have the will and skill to accept responsibility for the diverse individuals we teach?
   • To develop positive ties with students to encourage their growth
   • To see their dreams and uncertainties
   • To study and respond to their cultures
   • To work with students to build positive learning communities
2. Do we have a vision of the power of high-quality learning to help young people build lives?
   • To know what really matters in the discipline
   • To ensure student understanding of what matters most
   • To discover what's relevant and compelling to individuals
   • To build student engagement in learning

3. Are we willing to do the work of building bridges of possibility between what we teach and the diverse learners we teach?
- To seek out students' strengths and deficiencies
- To develop flexible teaching routines
- To create learning options for varied needs
- To coach for success
- To monitor individual growth against goals

That is the essence of expert teaching. It dignifies our work and our profession—even as it dignifies the students we teach.

To Learn More About It . . .

Many excellent sources describe more about instructional strategies that support the learning of a wide range of students. Here are a few:

Instructional Strategies Online (Saskatoon Public School Division)
http://olc.spsd.sk.ca/DE/PD/instr/instrsk.html

Includes information on concept maps, graphic organizers, Jigsaw, learning contracts, literature circles, RAFT, Readers' Theater, response journals, structured controversy, story mapping, synectics, Think-Pair-Share, Web quests, word walls, and other strategies.

University of Virginia, Curry School of Education Reading Quest
http://curry.edschool.virginia.edu/go/readquest/strat/

Includes information on carousel brainstorming, clock buddies, column notes, graphic organizers, history frames, inquiry charts, KWL, opinion-proof, questioning the author, RAFTs, selective highlighting, Think-Pair-Share, 3-2-1 summaries, word maps, and other strategies.

English Companion Web Site (Jim Burke)
http://www.englishcompanion.com

Includes information on a variety of graphic organizers to support student thinking and understanding, engaging student thinking with images, modeling, structured collaboration, learning with your hands, reciprocal teaching, multiple means to deliver instruction, using student examples, involving students in assessment, using visual aids to improve instruction, visual thinking, and other strategies.

Fulfilling the Promise of the Differentiated Classroom: Strategies and Tools for Responsive Teaching by Carol Ann Tomlinson (ASCD, 2003)

Contains a toolbox of examples of instructional strategies used to engage a wide range of learners with important ideas and enduring understandings, including learning profile surveys, interest surveys, skills checklists, rubrics, student planning guides, step-by-step checklists, concepts walls, concept maps, peer review guides, learning menus, evaluation checklists, Think-Tac-Toe, RAFTs, tiering, Complex Instruction, ThinkDots, and other strategies.

Time for Literacy Centers: How to Organize and Differentiate Instruction by Gretchen Owocki (Heinemann, 2005)

What Are the Other Kids Doing While You Teach Small Groups? by Donna Marriott (Creative Teaching Press, 1997)

Winning Strategies for Classroom Management by Carol Cummings (ASCD, 2000)

Note

1. As we have noted, exceptions to this premise occur when some students with severe cognitive disability require IEPs that deviate consistently and pervasively from the general curriculum because they are unable to engage with the key ideas of content.

5.

CONSIDERING EVIDENCE OF LEARNING IN DIVERSE CLASSROOMS

What should count as evidence of learning? Of understanding?
How might we differentiate our assessments without sacrificing validity and reliability?
How can we maintain standards without standardization?
How can assessment promote learning, not simply measure it?

Anyone concerned about teaching and learning is automatically interested in assessment. Assessment provides us with evidence to help answer important questions: "Did the student learn it?" "To what extent does the student understand?" "How might I adjust my teaching to be more effective for learners with varying needs?" The logic of backward design signals the importance of "thinking like an assessor" by placing Stage 2 (determining acceptable evidence) *before* Stage 3 (planning teaching and learning activities). By considering in advance the assessment evidence needed to validate that the desired results have been achieved, teaching becomes more purposeful and focused. Also, with clarity about what constitutes evidence that students have achieved desired results, teachers have a consistent framework within which they can make modifications for their students' readiness levels, interests, and learning preferences.

Principles of Effective Assessment

Three key principles should inform and guide classroom assessment. We'll now explore their conceptual foundation and consider the practical applications of each within academically diverse classrooms. Each of the principles provides a rationale for attending to student variance within the parameters of best practice.

Assessment Principle 1: Consider Photo Albums Versus Snapshots

Assessment is a process by which we make inferences about what students know, understand, and can do based on information obtained through assessment. Although educators sometimes loosely refer to an assessment as being valid and reliable, in fact a more precise conception has to do with the extent to which the results of an assessment permit valid and reliable inferences. Because all forms of assessment have inherent measurement error, our inferences are more dependable when we consider more than one measure. In other words, reliable assessment demands multiple sources of evidence.

Consider this principle in terms of a photographic analogy. A photo album typically contains a number of pictures taken over time in different contexts. When viewed as a whole, the album presents a more accurate and revealing "portrait" of an individual than does any single snapshot within. It is the same with classroom assessment—a single test at the end of instruction is less likely to provide a complete picture of a student's learning than a collection of diverse sources of evidence is.

Professional measurement specialists (psychometricians) understand this basic assessment principle. For example, Dr. Michael Kean (1994), vice president for CTB/McGraw-Hill, a major publisher of standardized tests, states: "Multiple measures are essential because no one test can do it all. Therefore, no test, no matter how good it is, should be the sole criterion for any decision."

Unfortunately, most politically driven accountability systems in North America rely on "quick and dirty" standardized tests (which provide a snapshot rather than a photo album) as a basis for judging students, schools, and districts. There is nothing inherently wrong with standardized tests. They provide useful and comparable data about student achievement levels on easily tested content goals. However, the problem occurs when the results of a *single* test are used to make high-stakes decisions. The widespread use of one-shot accountability testing has consequences that are well documented and include the following:

• The pressures to improve test scores can lead to a narrowing of the curriculum toward the tested topics and an overemphasis on "test prep" at the expense of meaningful learning.

• Important educational goals that are not easily and cheaply tested in a large-scale context (e.g., oral communication, decision making, research, expression in the arts) can fall through the cracks if they are not measured.

• The standardized nature of most large-scale, "one-size-fits-all" testing flies in the face of what we know (i.e., not every child learns in the same way at the same time).

• The predominant assessment format (selected-response) favors students with facility for recall and recognition. The results of high-pressure exams in which reading ability is paramount may present a distorted picture of the achievement of learners whose parents do not speak standard English, as well as of students with disabilities.

The overreliance on a single measure as a basis for inferences and high-stakes decisions is psychometrically unsound and politically risky, as recent testing scandals attest (Hendrie, 2002; White, 1999). However, our focus is less about the ills of accountability testing than it is about those aspects of assessment that we can influence—the assessments that we use in our classrooms, schools, and districts.

It is in the context of the classroom that the application of "assessment as photo album" is most feasible and natural. Indeed, a variety of classroom assessments may be used to gather evidence of learning (McTighe & Wiggins, 2004):

• Selected-response format (e.g., multiple-choice, true-false) quizzes and tests
• Written or oral responses to academic prompts (short-answer format)
• Performance assessment tasks, yielding
    – Extended written products (e.g., essays, lab reports)
    – Visual products (e.g., PowerPoint shows, murals)
    – Oral performances (e.g., oral reports, foreign-language dialogues)
    – Demonstrations (e.g., skill performances in physical education)

- Long-term, "authentic" projects (e.g., senior exhibitions)
- Portfolios (systematic collections of student work over time)
- Reflective journals or learning logs
- Informal, ongoing observations of students (e.g., teacher note taking, probing questions, exit cards, Quick-Writes)
- Formal observations of students using observable indicators or criterion list
- Student self-assessments
- Peer reviews and peer response groups

In planning for classroom assessments, consider the "photo album" graphic organizer in Figure 5.1. This figure illustrates the use of multiple sources of evidence for assessing attainment of an important content standard, in this case arithmetic problem solving. Although we are not suggesting that *everything* we teach requires multiple assessments, we do believe that more than a single source of evidence is needed for our significant, "essential and enduring" goals. That recommendation may mean providing more than one format option for key assessments. It will certainly mean varying format options over the course of a unit of study. Both are clearly important in academically diverse classrooms where different students will most fully be able to demonstrate their knowledge, understanding, and skill in different formats.

Although useful for individual planning, this graphic organizer has proven especially valuable for team planning. As suggested in Chapter 3, the logic of backward design dictates that evidence of learning (Stage 2) must be derived from the desired results (Stage 1), and this logic applies to teachers working in grade-level and department teams as well. In standards-based education, the rubber meets the road with assessment. Unless we agree not only on the goals but also on the needed assessment evidence of meeting them, we cannot claim that our teaching is standards based. By working with colleagues to forge consensus about what it looks like when students achieve desired results, educators realize more coherent curricula, more reliable assessments, and greater consistency in grading and reporting *across* classrooms and schools.

Including a variety of assessments is important not only from a measurement perspective but as a matter of sensitivity to varied learners. Because students differ in their preferred way of showing what they have learned, providing multiple and various assessment types increases the opportunity for students to work to their strengths and, ultimately, the likelihood of their success. Like the judicial system, we need a "preponderance of evidence" to convict students of learning! Ultimately, the validity and reliability of our

FIGURE 5.1
An Assessment Photo Album

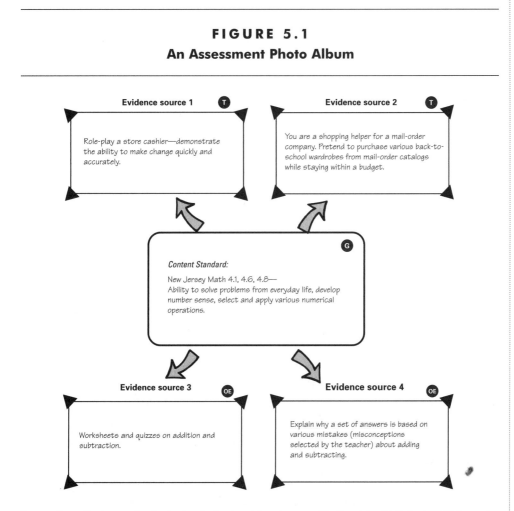

Evidence source 1 (T)

Role-play a store cashier—demonstrate the ability to make change quickly and accurately.

Evidence source 2 (T)

You are a shopping helper for a mail-order company. Pretend to purchase various back-to-school wardrobes from mail-order catalogs while staying within a budget.

(G)

Content Standard:

New Jersey Math 4.1, 4.6, 4.8—
Ability to solve problems from everyday life, develop number sense, select and apply various numerical operations.

Evidence source 3 (OE)

Worksheets and quizzes on addition and subtraction.

Evidence source 4 (OE)

Explain why a set of answers is based on various mistakes (misconceptions selected by the teacher) about adding and subtracting.

Source: From Understanding by Design Professional Development Workbook (p. 146), by J. McTighe and G. Wiggins, 2004, Alexandria, VA: Association for Supervision and Curriculum Development. Copyright 2004 by the Association for Supervision and Curriculum Development. Adapted with permission.

judgments about student achievement are enhanced when we ensure that the types of assessment we use are effective for particular learners in providing evidence of their achievement.

Assessment Principle 2: Match the Measures with the Goals

To allow valid inferences to be drawn from the results, an assessment must provide an appropriate measure of a given goal. Thus, thinking about assessment evidence in Stage 2 cannot be done without a careful consideration of the desired results (Stage 1). We have found it useful to distinguish among three types of educational goals: (1) *declarative knowledge*—what students should know and understand, (2) *procedural knowledge*—what students should be able to do, and (3) *dispositions*—what attitudes or habits of mind students should display (Marzano, 1992). These categories have direct implications for how we teach and assess. For example, if we want to see whether students know multiplication tables or chemical symbols *(declarative knowledge)*, then objective test items, such as multiple-choice, matching, true-false, or fill-in-the-blank, will provide the appropriate evidence in an efficient manner. When we wish to check for proficiency in skill/process areas such as drawing, writing, or driving *(procedural knowledge)*, some type of performance assessment is needed. For *dispositions,* such as "appreciation of the arts" or "persistence," evidence will have to be collected over time through observations, examples, portfolios, and self-assessments. After all, a quiz on "persistence" would be an inappropriate measure of such a goal.

In a differentiated classroom, there is particular meaning in attending to student proficiency with all three kinds of knowledge. Some students will need additional support, for example, with the procedural knowledge (skills) in a unit but be progressing well with the declarative (knowledge and understanding), whereas others will exhibit the reverse profile at a given time. If a teacher is to use assessment data to map instructional plans, it matters that the data provide information on student strengths and needs with essential knowledge, understanding, and skill. Without using such individual-specific data, we give ourselves permission to teach in a one-size-fits-all fashion—asking the impossible of some students while teaching others what they already know (Taba & Elkins, 1966). In addition, data on student dispositions or habits of mind and work can yield important insights about why a particular student is (or is not) progressing at a given time. Furthermore, data on student dispositions becomes important in reporting student progress in a differentiated classroom. This topic will be discussed further in Chapter 8.

Diversity of goals implies that we should include a variety of assessment pictures in our assessment "photo album." We accomplish this by selecting various assessment formats to give us appropriate measures for our goals. Yet, despite the importance of collecting multiple pieces of evidence and matching the measures with goals, we often observe teachers making assessment decisions based on what assessment is easiest to give and grade. This is understandable given the time- and labor-intensiveness of some types of assessment and the pressures to "defend" grades to students, parents, and administrators. Nevertheless, we strongly recommend that our goals should dictate the nature of our assessments, not external factors. It is incumbent upon school and district leaders to establish structures (e.g., time for group scoring of student work and realistic report card completion timelines) so that responsible assessment practices can be enacted feasibly.

Assessing Understanding

In Chapter 3, we discussed the value of identifying the "big ideas" that we want students to come to understand. Now, we'll take a finer-grained look at this particular goal of "understanding" by examining three questions: What is the difference between knowing and understanding? How will we know that students *truly* understand the big ideas that we have identified? How might we allow students to demonstrate their understanding in diverse ways without compromising standards?

Knowing is binary—you either know something or you don't. Declarative knowledge of facts and basic concepts falls into this category, and assessing such factual knowledge can be readily accomplished through objective tests and quizzes featuring "correct" answers. Understanding is more a matter of degree, as our language suggests. For example, we speak of someone having a sophisticated insight, a solid grasp, an incomplete or naive conception, or a misunderstanding. Thus, when we ask, "To what extent does she understand?" the answer is revealed along a continuum as shades of gray, rather than black and white. This point has implications for how we assess and how we describe the results.

A challenge for assessing understanding is found in the word itself—understand has different connotations. For instance, consider these four uses of the term:

- They really *understand* Spanish.
- She *understands* what I am going through.
- He knows the historical facts but does not *understand* their significance for today.
- I now *understand* that I never saw the big picture.

The first example suggests that understanding a language enables someone to *use* it—that is, to communicate effectively via listening, speaking, reading, and writing. In the second example, the emphasis is on *empathy*—the capacity to feel as someone else. The third case implies *transfer*—the ability to apply what one has learned in a new situation. The fourth example is *metacognitive;* that is, the individual is capable of reflecting on his or her thinking and learning processes.

The fact that the term *understand* can be used in such diverse ways has led some researchers and educators to decry its use in framing goals. They argue that it is too ambiguous to provide goal clarity and measurement specificity.

Taking a different tack, Wiggins and McTighe (1998, 2005) propose that these various connotations can be used to formulate a conception of understanding for assessment purposes. They propose that understanding is revealed through six facets, summarized in Figure 5.2.

These six facets do not present a theory of how people come to understand something. We'll leave that to the cognitive psychologists to explain. Instead, the facets are intended to serve as *indicators* of how understanding is revealed. Thus, they provide guidance as to the kinds of assessments we need to determine the extent of student understanding.

Although the six facets offer a full array of possible indicators of understanding, a basic approach for determining whether learners really understand involves two: explain and apply. When we speak of explanation, we seek more than a memorized recitation. Doctoral students are required to *defend* their dissertation in order to demonstrate to their committee that they understand their research and its meaning. The same idea applies, albeit in a less formalized manner, when we ask learners to "put it in their own words,"

FIGURE 5.2
The Six Facets of Understanding

When we truly understand, we

• Can **explain** via generalizations or principles: provide justified and systematic accounts of phenomena, facts, and data; make insightful connections and provide illuminating examples or illustrations.

• Can **interpret:** tell meaningful stories; offer apt translations; provide a revealing historical or personal dimension to ideas and events; make it personal or accessible through images, anecdotes, analogies, and models.

• Can **apply:** effectively use and adapt what we know in diverse and real contexts—we can "do" the subject.

• Have **perspective:** see and hear points of view through critical eyes and ears; see the big picture.

• Display **empathy:** find value in what others might find odd, alien, or implausible; perceive sensitively on the basis of prior direct experience.

• Have **self-knowledge:** show metacognitive awareness; perceive the personal style, prejudices, projections, and habits of mind that both shape and impede our own understanding; be aware of what we do not understand; reflect on the meaning of learning and experience.

give reasons for their answers, support their position, justify their solution, and show their work.

It is important to note that explanations need not be exclusively verbal (written or oral). Visual explanations in the form of concept maps, sequence chains, flowcharts, visual analogies, and so on, can be quite revealing and may be particularly beneficial in ensuring that students who have strong visual preferences or who struggle with verbal expression have an opportunity to express what they are learning.

When we call for application, we do not mean a mechanical response or mindless "plug-in" of a memorized formula. Rather, we ask students to transfer—to use what they know in a new situation. We recommend that teachers set up realistic, authentic contexts for assessment; when students are able to apply their learning thoughtfully and flexibly, true understanding is demonstrated. Consider an analogy here. In team sports, coaches routinely conduct drills to develop and refine basic skills. However, these practice drills are always purposefully pointed toward performance in the game. Too often, we find that classrooms overemphasize decontextualized drills and provide too few opportunities for students to actually "play the game." Figure 5.3 differentiates between inauthentic drills and authentic application.

FIGURE 5.3
Inauthentic Versus Authentic Work

Inauthentic Work	Authentic Work
Fill in the blank	Conduct research using primary sources
Select an answer from given choices	Debate a controversial issue
Answer recall questions at end of chapter	Conduct a scientific investigation
Solve contrived problems	Solve "real-world" problems
Practice decontextualized skills	Interpret literature
Diagram sentences	Do purposeful writing for an audience

Both drills and authentic application are necessary in the field and the classroom. Students need to master the basics, and skill drills support that need. But learners also need a chance to use their knowledge and skills—in other words, to "do" the subject.

When students can apply knowledge and skill appropriately to a new situation and can effectively explain *how* and *why*, we have the evidence to "convict" them of understanding.

Let's consider two examples of assessment tasks that require application and explanation for a middle grades unit on nutrition.

• Because our class has been learning about nutrition, 2nd grade teachers in our school have asked for our help in teaching their students about good eating. Create an illustrated brochure to teach the 2nd graders about the importance of good nutrition for healthful living. Use cut-out pictures of food and original drawings to show the difference between a balanced diet and an unhealthy diet. Show at least two health problems that can occur as a result of poor eating. Your brochure should also contain accurate information and should be easy for 2nd graders to read and understand.

• Because we have been learning about nutrition, the camp director at the Outdoor Educational Center has asked us to propose a nutritionally balanced menu for our three-day trip to the center later this year. Using the USDA Food Pyramid guidelines and the nutrition facts on food labels, design a plan for three days, including the three main meals and three snacks (morning, afternoon, and campfire). Your goal: a healthy and tasty menu. In addition to your menu, prepare a letter to the director explaining how your menu meets the USDA nutritional guidelines. Include a chart showing a breakdown of the fat, protein, and carbohydrate content and vitamins, minerals, and calories. Finally, explain how you have tried to make your menu tasty enough for your fellow students to want to eat.

Notice that in both examples, students are asked to apply their knowledge of nutrition to a real-world situation and include an explanation. They are required to use what they know in flexible ways to meet a goal for an identified audience. Both tasks are open-ended in that they allow students to personalize their response while still meeting established criteria—an example of standards without standardization. Such assessments provide evidence of meaningful learning in a qualitatively different way than would an objective test of nutrition facts (although we might well include such a test as part of our photo album). Certainly, in a differentiated classroom a teacher acknowledges that although it is not negotiable that a student demonstrate understanding, how that student might best do so *is* highly flexible. Furthermore, it is quite possible that some students will be appropriately challenged by an assessment task that is more complex and requires more advanced manipulation of skills, whereas other students need a task that is more concrete and requires a more fundamental, foundational, or familiar application of skills. That the students must show understanding of essential big ideas does not vary, but the "degree of difficulty" of the assessment task can vary to appropriately address variety in learner readiness.

The GRASPS Frame

As a means of creating more authentic "performances of understanding," we recommend that teachers frame assessment tasks with the features suggested by the acronym GRASPS. In other words, include (1) a real-world **goal,** (2) a meaningful **role** for the student, (3) authentic (or simulated) real-world **audience(s),** (4) a contextualized **situation** that involve real-world application, (5) student-generated culminating **products** and performances, and (6) consensus-driven performance **standards** (criteria) for judging success. Notice these elements in the two previously presented examples.

We do not mean to imply that *everything* we teach or assess needs to be framed using GRASPS. However, for those important ideas and processes that you really want students to understand, we believe that more authentic tasks have merit. Performance tasks having these features provide meaningful learning targets for learners, worthy performance goals for teaching, and the kind of evidence needed to assess true understanding.

Moreover, it is important to stress that virtually all students in our schools should have regular opportunities to demonstrate their proficiency with important content goals through assessments that embody the GRASPS characteristics. Some parameters for student work and teacher scaffolding of student success may well need to vary among students, but not the opportunity to express learning through meaningful assessments that include student choice, that are focused on essential content goals, and that are judged according to substantive criteria. A highly advanced learner, for example, may apply understandings in a less familiar or less well-defined context or for an audience with sophisticated knowledge of the domain in question. A student who struggles to learn may apply understandings in a more familiar or more structured context or for an audience of peers or younger students. Both students should be expected to demonstrate genuine understanding of essential principles in real-world situations.

Assessment Principle 3: Form Follows Function

The way in which we design and use classroom assessments should be directly influenced by the answers to four questions: What are we assessing? Why are we assessing? For whom are the results intended? How will the results be used? We have discussed the relationship between what and how we assess in the previous section. Now we turn our attention to purpose.

Classroom assessments serve different purposes, one of which is summative. *Summative* assessments are generally used to summarize what has been learned. These assessments tend to be evaluative in nature, and their results are often encapsulated and reported as a score or a grade. Familiar examples of summative assessments include tests, performance tasks, final exams, culminating projects, and work portfolios. These evaluative assessments command the attention of students and parents, because their results typically "count" and become recorded on report cards and transcripts.

In addition to evaluation, two other assessment purposes—diagnostic and formative—are critical to teaching and learning. *Diagnostic* assessments (or pre-assessments) typically precede instruction and are used to check students' prior knowledge and skill levels and identify misconceptions, interests, or learning style preferences. They provide information to assist teacher planning and guide differentiated instruction. Examples of diagnostic assessments include skill checks, knowledge surveys, nongraded pre-tests, interest or learning preference checks, and checks for misconceptions.

Formative assessments occur concurrently with instruction. These ongoing assessments provide information to guide teaching and learning for improving achievement. Formative assessments include both formal and informal methods, such as ungraded quizzes, oral questioning, observations, draft work, think-alouds, student-constructed concept maps, dress rehearsals, peer response groups, and portfolio reviews.

Although summative/evaluative assessments often receive the most attention, diagnostic and formative assessments provide critical "along the way" information to guide instruction in response to the nature and needs of the diverse learners. Waiting until the end of teaching to find out how well students have learned is simply too late. Just as the most successful coaches and sponsors of extracurricular activities such as yearbook, orchestra, theater, and athletics recognize the importance of ongoing assessments and continuous adjustments as the means to achieve maximum performance, so do the best teachers. As a validation of good instincts, recent research has confirmed the benefits of regular use of diagnostic and formative assessments as feedback for learning (Black & William, 1998). In a differentiated classroom, a teacher continuously examines ongoing assessment data for individuals as a means of adapting "up-front" teaching plans so that they address particular learner needs. As noted educator Hilda Taba pointed out,

"Diagnosis, of course, is never completed. Every contact with students reveals something that the teacher did not know before, something important for intelligent planning of instruction" (Taba & Elkins, 1966, p. 24).

Responsive Assessment to Promote Learning in Diverse Classrooms

We conclude this chapter by describing four classroom assessment practices that honor student differences and promote learning.

Assess *Before* Teaching

Diagnostic assessment (pre-assessment) is as important to teaching as a physical exam is to prescribing appropriate medical regimens. At the outset of any unit of study, some students are likely already to have mastered many of the skills that the teacher is about to "introduce," and they may already have a relatively sophisticated understanding of some or all of the unit's enduring understandings. Simultaneously, some students are likely to be deficient in precursor skills necessary to become proficient with the unit's essential skills and to lack a context or experience base for beginning a study of the unit's enduring understandings. A teacher who intends to support success for each learner needs a sense of the learners' starting points as a unit begins. "Teaching in the dark is questionable practice" (Taba & Elkins, 1966).

Pre-assessments should focus on the unit's essential knowledge, understanding, and skill. They should provide a window into important strengths and weaknesses that students may bring to the study. Furthermore, they should not be graded. Rather, pre-assessments contribute to a teacher's general sense of each student's readiness status relative to essential content goals for the unit. At key points in the year, pre-assessments may also be useful in gaining insights about a student's interests or preferred routes to learning. Many formats are useful for pre-assessment, including 3-2-1 cards, Frayer diagrams, quizzes, journal entries, checklists, and concept maps.

Informed with a sense of students' varying learning needs, a teacher can begin to form instructional groups, assign appropriate student tasks, locate appropriate learning materials, and so on. Then, throughout the unit, formative assessments continue to assist the teacher in refining his or her understanding of a learner's needs and in responding to learners in ways likely to maximize their growth.

Offer Appropriate Choices

Responsiveness in assessment is as important as it is in teaching. Just as students differ in their preferred ways of taking in and processing information, so do they vary in the manner by which they best show what they have learned. Some students need to "do," whereas others thrive on oral explanations. Some excel at visual representations; others are adept at writing. To make valid inferences about learning, teachers need to allow students to work to their strengths. A totally standardized, one-size-fits-all approach to classroom assessment may be efficient, but it is not "fair," because any chosen format will favor some students and penalize others.

Assessment becomes responsive when students are given appropriate options for demonstrating knowledge, skill, and understanding. In other words, allow some choices—but always with the intent of collecting *needed evidence based on goals*. Without a clear connection between the desired results and the required evidence, teachers will be stuck assessing apples, oranges, and grapes.

An adaptation of tic-tac-toe provides a structure for giving students choices of products and performances while keeping the end in mind. Figure 5.4 illustrates one example in which the teacher structures product and performance options of various genres by which students could display their content understanding.

The tic-tac-toe format enables teachers to structure the options while giving the students choices. The choice options are flexible. For example, if we want students to write, then we would ask all learners to choose one option from the first column and then one other product/performance from the second or third columns. If we seek an accurate and complete explanation, we might give students greater freedom to choose options from the other columns. Figure 5.5 shows a tic-tac-toe chart with greater openness. The "FREE" blocks allow students to propose an alternative source of evidence that suits their strength. For a major project, we might allow students to produce three products, picking one from each column.

FIGURE 5.4
Product and Performance Tic-Tac-Toe (Version 1)

Written	Visual	Oral
Research report	Poster	Lesson presentation
News article	Graphic organizer	Oral presentation
Information brochure	PowerPoint	Radio interview

FIGURE 5.5
Product and Performance Tic-Tac-Toe (Version 2)

Written	Visual	Oral
FREE	Poster	Speech
Persuasive essay	FREE	Debate
Editorial	Campaign poster	FREE

Regardless of how open-ended the task and how many product/performance options are provided, it is imperative that we identify a *common* set of evaluative criteria. This advice might seem counterintuitive; that is, how can we have the *same* criteria if we give students *different* product options? The answer goes back to the logic of UbD's backward design. The general assessment evidence we need to collect in Stage 2 is determined by the desired results identified in Stage 1. However the particulars of an assessment task may be structured so as to allow student choice as discussed earlier. For example, within a unit on nutrition we want students to show their understanding of a balanced diet. This understanding could be assessed by a task that asks students to explain the concept and offer an illustrative example, and the needed evidence could be obtained in writing, orally, or visually. However, regardless of the response mode, all students would be judged by a rubric containing the following key criteria connected to the content: *clear, accurate,* and *complete explanation* of "balanced diet," with an *appropriate example* that *illustrates* the concept. In other words, the criteria are derived primarily from the content goal, not the response mode.

Now, we may wish to add student-specific criteria for the needs of particular learners. For instance, a teacher may stress the use of primary resources in research work undertaken by a highly able 4th grader, whereas secondary sources are appropriate for other learners in the class. (This illustration assumes that use of primary sources is *not* a content goal for the unit.) Likewise, a teacher may add product-specific criteria for the different product genres. For example, if a student prepares a poster to illustrate a balanced diet, we could look for *neatness, composition,* and effective use of *color.* Likewise, if a student made an oral presentation, we could judge her *pronunciation, delivery rate,* and *eye contact* with the audience. However, in this example we consider these to be secondary criteria linked to specific products/performances, rather than the key criteria determined by the content goal. (Note that a speech teacher would use the last set of criteria as key because of their importance to the content standard of effective speaking.)

Of course, we want students to do quality work, regardless of what options they select. But more important, we need to employ the criteria called for by the content goals. If we vary *these* key criteria for different students based on the products they select, then we no longer have a valid and reliable assessment measure. See Figure 5.6 for a visual summary of these points.

We conclude this section with three cautions. First, we must always keep in mind that our aim is to collect appropriate evidence of learning based on the goals, not to simply offer a "cool" menu of product possibilities. If a content standard calls for proficiency in writing or oral presentation, it would be inappropriate to provide alternative performance options other than writing or speaking—except in cases of students for whom writing or speaking is inordinately difficult because of disabilities.

FIGURE 5.6
Criteria and Differentiated Assessments

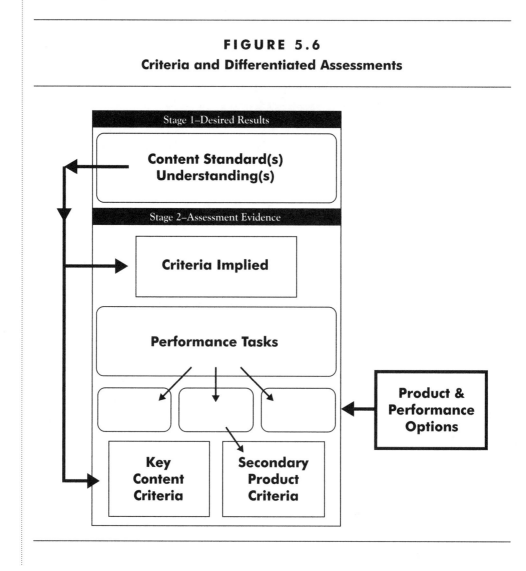

Second, the options we provide must be worth the time and energy required. It would be inefficient to have students develop an elaborate three-dimensional display or an animated PowerPoint show for content that could be efficiently and appropriately assessed with a multiple-choice quiz. In the folksy words of a teacher friend, "The juice must be worth the squeeze."

Third, feasibility must be considered. Ideally, we might wish to individualize all major assignments and performance assessments, but realistically we have only so much time and energy. Therefore, educators must be judicious in determining when it is important to offer product and performance options (and how many should be offered), striking a balance between a single path and a maze of options.

Despite the challenges, we believe that efforts to provide options for assessment are well worth the trouble. Students given appropriate choices on respectful tasks are more likely to put forth effort and feel a genuine sense of accomplishment for a job well done.

Provide Feedback Early and Often

Legendary football coach Vince Lombardi summed it up: "Feedback is the breakfast of champions." All types of learning, whether on the practice field or in the classroom, require feedback. Ironically, the high-quality feedback systems necessary to enhance learning are limited in our schools, at least in academic classrooms. Consider the observations of assessment expert Grant Wiggins (1998):

> If I had to summarize what I have seen over the past decade in all kinds of schools (public and private; elementary, secondary and collegiate; with and without state testing programs), I would have to report that many educators seem to believe that feedback means giving lots of approval, and some disapproval and advice. In classrooms, the most common piece of so-called feedback is "Good job!" or some equivalent phrase.
>
> It is, of course, important to praise students because it often satisfies and encourages them, but it cannot help them to improve their performance. Praise keeps you in the game; real feedback helps you get better. Feedback tells you what you did or did not do and enables you to self adjust. Indeed, the more self-evident feedback, the more autonomy the performer develops, and vice-versa. (p. 46)

Four qualities characterize an effective feedback system. The feedback must (1) be timely, (2) be specific, (3) be understandable to the receiver, and (4) allow for adjustment. Waiting three weeks (or three months) to find out how you did on a standardized test will not help your learning. Learners need to find out promptly their strengths and weaknesses in order to improve. The greater the delay, the less likely it is that the feedback will be helpful or used.

Not surprisingly, the best feedback is often observed in the "performance-based" subjects such as art, music, drama, speech, vocational and technical education, family and consumer sciences, and physical education. We also see feedback effectively employed in athletics and extracurriculars, such as band, newspaper, and debate. Indeed, the essence of "coaching" involves ongoing assessment and feedback, as Lombardi's comment suggests.

Specificity is key to focused adjustment. Too many educators consider grades and scores as "feedback," when, in fact, they fail the specificity test. Pinning a letter (B-) or a number (82%) on a student's work is no more helpful than comments such as "Way to go" or "Try harder." Although good grades and positive remarks may feel good, they do not advance learning. Specific feedback sounds different—for example, "Your research paper is well organized and contains lots of specific information. You used multiple sources and documented them appropriately. However, your paper lacks a clear conclusion, and you never answered your basic research question." From this feedback, the report writer knows specifically where the paper is strong and what revisions are needed.

Because feedback is directed to the learner, it must be understood. Rubrics are often viewed as feedback tools and can indeed serve in this capacity. However, sometimes the language in a rubric can be lost on a student. Exactly what does the teacher mean by "elegant reasoning" or "sophisticated analysis"? If we want feedback to inform learners and guide their improvement, our feedback must be clear and comprehensible. One approach is to develop "kid language" rubrics. For instance, instead of "documents the reasoning process," we might say, "Show your work in a step-by-step manner so that others can see how you were thinking."

A second approach for making feedback understandable involves the use of models and exemplars. Experienced teachers have a clear conception of what we mean by "well organized," but there is no guarantee that the phrase will convey that same idea to students. They are more likely to understand our feedback when we show several examples that are well organized and easy to grasp compared with several that lack organization and are difficult to follow. If we expect students to act on our feedback, they have to understand it. The use of models helps to make the "invisible visible" through tangible examples. It is also possible to share with individuals or small groups of students exemplars of work completed by students who were at their approximate level of proficiency and who did—or did not—demonstrate proficiency in their work. In that way, students can see work that "looks like they might have done it" and simultaneously see examples of next steps in quality that they believe they could achieve with effort and support.

Here's a simple, straightforward test for a feedback system: Can the learners tell *specifically* from the given feedback what they have done well and what they could do next time to improve? If not, the feedback is not yet specific or understandable enough for the learner.

Finally, the learner needs opportunities to act on the feedback—to refine, revise, practice, and retry. Writers rarely compose a perfect manuscript on the first try, which is why the writing process stresses cycles of drafting, feedback (from self-assessment, peer review, and teacher comments), and revision as the route to excellence. The same process applies in any subject where the goal is deep understanding and fluent performance. Therefore, teachers should build into their instructional plans regular opportunities for feedback and refinement. Learning demands it.

Encourage Self-Assessment and Reflection

The most effective learners are metacognitive; that is, they are mindful of how they learn, set personal learning goals, regularly self-assess and adjust their performance, and use productive strategies to assist their learning. Less effective learners seem to go through school as if in a cloud. They seem clueless about their preferred learning style and about strategies that can enhance their achievement.

Research and experience have shown that metacognitive strategies can be taught, and the benefits to learners can be noteworthy (Bransford, Brown, & Cocking, 2000; Costa & Kallick, 2000; Flavell, 1985). One straightforward approach to cultivating metacognition involves having learners regularly respond to reflective questions such as those listed here (McTighe & Wiggins, 2004). Such questions encourage students to reflect on their learning, consider transfer possibilities, self-assess their performance, and set goals:

What do you really understand about _____ ?

What questions/uncertainties do you still have about _____ ?

What was most effective in _____?

What was least effective in _____?

How could you improve_____?

What would you do differently next time?

What are you most proud of?

What are you most disappointed in?

How difficult was _____ for you?

What are your strengths in _____?

What are your deficiencies in _____?

To what extent has your performance improved over time?

How does your preferred learning style influence _____?

What grade/score do you deserve? Why?

How does what you've learned connect to other learning?

How has what you've learned changed your thinking?

How does what you've learned relate to the present and future?

What follow-up work is needed?

Such self-assessment in a differentiated classroom also enables student and teacher to focus both on nonnegotiable goals for the class and personal or individual goals that are important for the development of each learner. For instance, if students had opportunities to reflect on the appropriateness of the degree of task difficulty for them, to name their particular strengths and weaknesses, to think about how their learning preferences work for and against them, and to set personal improvement goals, it is likely that they would have more ownership in both their learning and their classroom where the teacher works to understand and respond to their needs.

Another simple yet effective strategy for providing feedback while encouraging self-assessment and goal setting is to adjust the format of a rubric. Notice in Figure 5.7 that two small squares have been inserted in the bottom left and right corners of each box in an analytic rubric. The squares on the left side enable students to self-assess their performance according to the established criteria and performance levels *before* they turn in their work. The teacher then uses the right-side squares to evaluate. Ideally, the two judgments would be close. If not, the discrepancy raises an opportunity to discuss the criteria, expectations, and performance standards. Over time, teacher and student judgments tend to converge; in fact, it is not unusual to observe that students are sometimes "harder" on themselves than the teacher is! The goal, of course, is not to see who is "hardest" but for the student to become progressively more effective at honest self-appraisal and productive self-improvement.

Now have a look at the two rectangles below the rubric. The first allows the teacher, a peer, or the student to offer comments, provide feedback, or raise questions. The second box is intended for students to set goals or plan

FIGURE 5.7
Rubric Format for Feedback, Self-Assessment, and Goal Setting

	Title	Labels	Accuracy	Neatness
3	The graph contains a title that clearly tells what the data show.	All parts of the graph (units of measurement, rows, etc.) are correctly labeled.	All data are accurately represented on the path.	The graph is very neat and easy to read.
2	The graph contains a title that suggests what the data show.	Some parts of the graph are inaccurately labeled.	Data representation contains minor errors.	The graph is generally neat and readable.
1	The title does not reflect what the data show OR the title is missing.	The graph is incorrectly labeled OR labels are missing.	The data are inaccurately represented, contain major errors, OR are missing.	The graph is sloppy and difficult to read.

Comments:

Goals/Actions:

actions to improve their future performance based on the feedback from the rubric. Used in this way, the rubric moves from being simply an evaluation tool for "pinning a number" on kids to a practical and robust vehicle for feedback, self-assessment, and goal setting.

Educators who provide regular opportunities for learners to self-assess and reflect often report a change in the culture of the classroom. As one teacher put it, "My students have shifted from asking, 'What did I get?' or 'What are you going to give me?' to becoming increasingly capable of knowing how they are doing and what they need to do to improve."

A Final Thought

Effective assessment practice is a cornerstone of teaching individuals for understanding. Effective assessments serve not only as indicators of student understanding but as data sources enabling teachers to shape their practice in ways that maximize the growth of the varied learners they teach. Effective assessments are not only indicators of student success with content goals but a dynamic part of the instructional process. Furthermore, effective assessment practice not only measures students but assists them in becoming evaluators of their own learning.

6

RESPONSIVE TEACHING WITH UbD IN ACADEMICALLY DIVERSE CLASSROOMS

What should be the curricular "givens" in instructional planning?
How can teachers use classroom elements flexibly to support student success?
How can teachers make instructional planning more manageable and efficient?
How can teachers select instructional strategies that are responsive to student need?
How do teachers organize and manage their classrooms to support responsive instruction?

There comes a time in curriculum design when the teacher necessarily shifts from curriculum planning to delivery of the curriculum to the human beings whom we believe would benefit from learning it. In other words, with the curriculum design in mind, we must consider just how we carry out the plans we've made so that they work for each of our students.

In the case of UbD and DI, the two considerations—understanding-based curriculum and differentiated instruction—are inextricably linked, of course, and require a "duet of thinking" on the part of the teacher. What matters most for all my students to learn? What instructional sequence will maximize learning? How are my students as individuals faring as they attempt to make sense of the important ideas and use the important skills? Who needs my assistance to achieve understanding? How might I arrange classroom time and space to ensure those options? How will I ensure that my students and I are working as a team to benefit everyone in the class? What work will benefit some students as I work with others? How will I gather evidence of student success with the unit's essential goals?

Despite the many elements to which a teacher must attend, four over-arching and interrelated questions circulate in tandem in the teacher's mind and inform one another: Who are the students I will teach? What matters most for students to learn here (curriculum)? How must I teach to ensure that each student grows systematically toward attainment of the goal and moves beyond it when indicated (instruction)? How will I know who is successful and who is not yet successful with particular goals (assessment)?

The focus of this chapter is instructional decision making in a classroom built on the principles of backward design and differentiation. Nonetheless, we begin again with some shared beliefs about the nature of curriculum in academically diverse settings because this remains the compass of planning, and a flawed compass will result in predictably flawed outcomes for the students we teach.

Core Beliefs About Curriculum and Diverse Student Populations

UbD and DI share a set of core tenets reflected in the axioms and corollaries in Chapter 1 and in many other places throughout the book. At the outset of an exploration of instruction in a classroom using backward design, it is important again to make explicit some of the beliefs that shape our vision of effective classrooms. Four of those beliefs follow.

Virtually all students[1] should consistently experience curricula rooted in the important ideas of a discipline that requires them to make meaning of information and think at high levels. We do not subscribe to the practice of reserving meaning-driven, thought-based, application-focused curriculum for only a small proportion of learners. We have ample evidence that students whom we often think of as "low performing" fare better with rich, significant curriculum. Examining multiple sources of research evidence, one report concludes that students we consider to be low performers "increase their grasp of advanced skills at least as much as their high-achieving counterparts when both experience instruction aimed at meaning and understanding. And for both groups, this approach produces results superior to those of conventional practices" (Knapp, Shields, & Turnbull, 1992, p. 27).

Effectively differentiated classrooms are developed to ensure all students have access to high-quality, meaning-focused curriculum. The belief that quality curriculum is rooted in the important ideas of a discipline is core to

UbD. That such curriculum belongs to virtually all students is a reflection of the key principle of "respectful teaching" in differentiation.

Students need opportunities to learn the "basics" and opportunities to apply them in meaningful ways. Too often, lower-achieving learners are relegated to a steady curricular diet of low-level skill drills and rote learning of facts. Although "the basics" are necessary for academic development, they are not sufficient. It is imperative that teachers help students recognize that these fundamentals serve larger purposes. Our colleague Grant Wiggins uses a coaching analogy to remind educators of the important relationship between means and ends. A good coach has players do sideline drills—but inevitably in service of playing the game. Few athletes would endlessly block a sled, practice corner kicks, or rehearse fast breaks if they didn't see the connection with the game they will play on Saturday. We believe students must develop essential skills, but they must do so in the context of preparing for a game in which they will play very shortly. Differentiation suggests that all learners will need to take part, at some times, in "sideline drills" as a means of refining and extending key skills. At certain times, sideline drills will be helpful for the development of particular students (just as effective coaches differentiate their practices based on a player's position and need). But all students should be first and foremost "players in the real game," and they should always see the immediate connection between a sideline drill and the game. It should never be the case that some students are consigned to sideline drills while others consistently play the game.

There is a need for balance between student construction of meaning and teacher guidance. We agree that students must make meaning for themselves. It cannot be imposed on them. The UbD emphasis on "uncoverage" of meaning (vs. "coverage" of the content) arises from our awareness that understanding must be constructed by the individual. Differentiation reminds us that different individuals will construct meaning from their differing experiences, abilities, and interests—and along different timetables and with different support systems. We are advocates for constructivism, but we also understand the teacher's essential role in helping students construct meaning. As a noted cognitive psychologist points out:

> A common misconception regarding "constructivist" theories of knowing is that teachers should never tell students anything directly but instead should allow them to construct knowledge for themselves. This perspective confuses a theory of

pedagogy (teaching) with a theory of knowing. There are times, usually after people have first grappled with issues on their own, that "teaching by telling" might work extremely well. (Bransford, Brown, & Cocking, 2000, p. 11)

We agree, and we encourage teachers to balance student opportunities to make sense of the big ideas of content, to monitor the evolution of student understandings, and to engage in teacher-guided student reflection on and direct instruction related to the enduring understandings.

In his book *The Paideia Proposal*, Mortimer Adler (1982) proposes three key instructional roles for teachers: direct instructor, facilitator, and coach. Figure 6.1 provides examples of teaching strategies related to each role. Many other strategies could be added to the list, but the important point is that the most effective teachers will balance these roles by purposefully using a variety of strategies in service of student understanding and maximum growth. Differentiation reminds us that there will be times when a strategy can be used effectively in the same way with an entire class, times when use of the strategy needs to be differentiated in order to be used effectively with the whole class, and times when particular strategies may be especially helpful in supporting the developing understanding of particular students or small groups of students. It is certainly the case that a teacher in a differentiated classroom develops a repertoire of instructional approaches aimed at maximizing the success of all learners. As one expert in teaching diverse student populations noted, it takes a skilled teacher to use instructional strategies effectively to help varied learners transform pieces of knowledge and understanding into the webs that define educational success (Kameenui, Carnine, Dixon, Simmons, & Coyne, 2002).

Students need to know the learning goals of a unit or lesson and criteria for successfully demonstrating proficiency with the goals. There should be no mystery for students about either intended learning outcomes or what success in achieving those outcomes will look like. The three stages of backward design can assist teachers in remembering to address this principle. For example:

Stage 1
   • Share the content standards and desired learning outcomes with students at the start of the unit.

FIGURE 6.1

Instructional Strategies That Support Various Teacher Roles

What the teacher uses:	What students need to do:
Didactic/Direct Instruction	**Receive, take in, and respond**
• Demonstration/modeling	• Observe, attempt, practice, refine
• Lecture	• Listen, watch, take notes, question
• Questions (convergent)	• Answer, give responses
Facilitative/Constructivist Methods	**Construct, examine, and extend meaning**
• Concept attainment	• Compare, induce, define, generalize
• Cooperative learning	• Collaborate, support others, teach
• Discussion	• Listen, question, consider, explain
• Experimental inquiry	• Hypothesize, gather data, analyze
• Graphic representation	• Visualize, connect, map relationships
• Guided inquiry	• Question, research, conclude, support
• Problem-based learning	• Pose/define problems, solve, evaluate
• Questions (open-ended)	• Answer and explain, reflect, rethink
• Reciprocal teaching	• Clarify, question, predict, teach
• Simulation (e.g., mock trial)	• Examine, consider, challenge, debate
• Socratic seminar	• Consider, explain, challenge, justify
• Writing process	• Brainstorm, organize, draft, revise
Coaching	**Refine skills and deepen understanding**
• Feedback/conferencing	• Listen, consider, practice, retry, refine
• Guided practice	• Rethink, revise, reflect, refine, recycle through

Source: From *Understanding by Design* (pp. 159–160), by G. Wiggins and J. McTighe, 1998, Alexandria, VA: Association for Supervision and Curriculum Development. Copyright 1998 by the Association for Supervision and Curriculum Development. Adapted with permission.

• Post and review the essential questions that will be explored during the unit.

• List the important knowledge and skills to be learned.

Stage 2

• At the start of a new unit, present to the students the types of assessments that will show evidence of learning (and understanding) by the end of the unit.

• Share the culminating performance tasks and accompanying rubric(s) so students will know what will be expected and how their work will be judged.

• Show models of student work on similar tasks so students can see what quality work looks like.

Stage 3

• Explicitly connect for the students the learning experiences and direct instruction during the unit with the desired results, essential questions, and expected performances.

• Have students regularly reflect on what they are learning and how it will help them with upcoming performance tasks as well as in life and later in school.

We believe, then, that the segue from planning quality curriculum to implementing it responsively should proceed from a belief that virtually all students should work with the big ideas and essential skills of the topic, at high levels of thought on authentic tasks, with support for developing both understanding and skill, with opportunity to make personal meaning of important ideas, with teacher-guided instruction to ensure clarity of understanding, and with the student's full knowledge of learning goals and indicators of learner success. Those should be givens for whatever instructional plans we make. From that foundation—and consistently using pre-assessment and formative assessment data to guide teacher thinking—planning for differentiated instruction can proceed on sure footing.

Planning Instruction for Understanding in a Differentiated Classroom

Even in a classroom where student differences are of little importance in instructional planning, a new set of questions is required of teachers in moving from development of curricular plans to their implementation: How do I give directions for tasks? How will I know what students understand and can do? How do I keep their interest? How do I know when to start and stop the various segments of a plan? How do we transition from one part of a lesson to the next? How do I distribute resource materials? The issues are abundant even in one-size-fits-all settings. Making all the pieces work right is something like playing a game of Chinese checkers or chess.

When a teacher honors and intends to respond to individual variance, the game becomes three-dimensional. The questions become more complex: Once I understand what various students know, understand, and can do—and what they do not know, do not understand, and cannot do—how will I arrange my time and theirs to ensure their continued growth? How do I make sure students have resources that are right for their readiness needs, interests, or learning profile? How do I know when to start and stop the various segments of the plan for the class as a whole—and when I might need to extend a segment for particular learners who have deep interests or lingering needs related to that segment? How do I help students transition at different times for different purposes so that the class remains focused on the important work at hand? How do I give directions for multiple tasks efficiently and effectively? There is no single right answer to these questions. A teacher who seeks answers to them is something like a jazz musician. The teacher uses many elements and approaches—sometimes planned and sometimes improvisational—to convey the message of the melody. It takes practice to be a good jazz musician. From the practice grows knowledge of music theory, a good ear for what is going on around the musician, a sense of timing, sensitivity to the meanings of the music, a tolerance for ambiguity, and creativity. The jazz musician never loses the melody but expresses it in many ways.

That skill set is not unlike that of a teacher in a differentiated classroom whose instruction is both planned and improvisational. That teacher is always aware of the melody—the curriculum goals—but finds many different ways to the melody. From that teacher's sustained professional practice comes both implicit and explicit understanding of how learning works, a good ear for the people around the teacher and for the flow of the classroom, increasing sensitivity to the power of the "music" to touch young lives and empower them, a tolerance for ambiguity, and creativity necessary to discover yet again another way to express the melody—to link learners with meaning.

To attempt an analysis of all the elements in a differentiated classroom in a few pages would be the equivalent of teaching jazz in a few pages. Nonetheless, a look at some ways a teacher may think about responsive instruction to help students "relate to the melody" sheds some light on the jazz skills of the teacher who differentiates instruction. To that end, we'll take a brief look at using classroom elements flexibly to support student success, clustering learner needs to make instructional planning more efficient, selecting instructional strategies for responsive teaching, and asking important management questions to allow instructional flexibility.

Using Classroom Elements Flexibly as Tools for Effective Instruction

Classrooms contain a number of elements that can be used at the discretion of the teacher in different manners for different purposes. Among the classroom elements that teachers employ daily—and can manipulate to help achieve desired ends—are time, space, resources, student groupings, instructional or learning strategies, presentation or teaching strategies, and partnerships.

Teachers who understand those elements to be tools at their disposal ask, "How might I use these tools to ensure that each of my students achieves the greatest possible success with important academic outcomes?" Thinking about teaching in that way suggests that perhaps some students would learn better if they had more time to master a skill or achieve an understanding, and some students might learn better if they spent less time on a particular skill or understanding. Sometimes learning might proceed more effectively with students seated in triads of similar-readiness peers; at other times, learning might be more effective with students working in mixed-readiness quads. Figure 6.2 summarizes just a few of a myriad of ways in which teachers might flexibly use key classroom elements to address varied learner needs, thereby helping more students achieve greater degrees of success with the goals of high-quality curriculum.

FIGURE 6.2
Options for Flexible Use of Classroom Elements
to Address Learning Needs

Element	Examples of Flexible Use	Learner Need Addressed
Time	Negotiated delay of due dates/times for tasks	Helps students who give evidence of hard work on tasks but who work slowly or have skills difficulties
	Compacting or exempting students from work on which they show mastery	Allows advanced learners to cut through tedium and continue academic growth
	Using homework contracts or learning centers to help students work on deficits in precursor skills areas	Supports students who have gaps in background knowledge rather than assuming there's no time to help them catch up
Space	Creating a "quiet zone" in the room where noise and visual stimuli are minimal	Helps students who need to work quietly, who are easily distracted, or who have quick tempers and need a place to "get away"
	Posting/using several room arrangement charts to have students rearrange the room quickly	Enables teacher to easily use small groups, whole class, or individual work and move between teacher- and student-focused work; benefits all students

(Figure continued on next page)

FIGURE 6.2

Options for Flexible Use of Classroom Elements
to Address Learning Needs *(continued)*

Element	Examples of Flexible Use	Learner Need Addressed
Resources	"Collecting" textbooks of different readability levels	Supports access of all students to key materials at appropriate challenge level
	Bookmarking Web sites on key topics in languages other than English	Supports English language learners in gaining understanding about essential topics in their first language to support their work in English
	Using video and audio clips to teach	Supports visual or auditory understanding for students who struggle with print, have visual or auditory learning preferences, or benefit from practical applications of ideas/skills
Student Groupings	Using pre-assigned groups so students know by cue where to move in the room and who to sit with	Enables teacher to move students quickly among varied groups; benefits all learners
	Planning for like and unlike readiness, interest, and learning profile groups	Allows targeted instruction by readiness, extension of ideas by mixed readiness, exploration of shared interests, expansion of interests, comfortable working and expansion of work comfort zone

FIGURE 6.2

**Options for Flexible Use of Classroom Elements
to Address Learning Needs (continued)**

Element	Examples of Flexible Use	Learner Need Addressed
Teaching Strategies	Teaching with both part-to-whole and whole-to-part emphasis	Supports students who learn better in either way—and all students by showing connections and meaning
	Interspersing lecture with small-group discussions	Benefits students who need movement and talk, helps students clarify understanding, and allows more student participation
	Making connections with key ideas/skills and students' cultures and interests	Increases affiliation, relevance, and motivation for many learners
Learning Strategies	Providing practical, analytical, and creative options for student work	Supports growth for students with varied learning preferences
	Providing tiered practice and assessments	Allows students at full range of readiness levels to work successfully with essential ideas and skills
	Encouraging students to work alone or with a peer	Allows all students to work in ways that are efficient for them
	Using "expert groups" to help teach key ideas	Increases motivation for many students by allowing them to extend areas of interest or develop new ones and to have an audience for their ideas

(Figure continued on next page)

FIGURE 6.2

Options for Flexible Use of Classroom Elements
to Address Learning Needs (*continued*)

Element	Examples of Flexible Use	Learner Need Addressed
Teacher Partnerships	Having students perform any classroom functions that are not imperative for the teacher to perform	Benefits students who need to move and stay busy, students who want to develop leadership skills, and many students by building ownership in and contribution to group
	Surveying parents for insights into their students' interests, learning preferences, and needs	Benefits many students whose strengths and needs might be unnoticed—and many students by encouraging parent links with school
	Working with a differentiation partner	Allows the teacher to see students through the eyes of a colleague who shares occasional time in the classroom, efficiency of planning by sharing curriculum/lesson design, and efficiency of management and classroom routine from someone with different experiences; benefits all students and the teacher

Clustering Learner Needs to Make Instructional Planning More Efficient

An elementary teacher often teaches five or six subjects to 30 or more students. A secondary teacher has one or more preparations per day for as many as 160 students. In either case, the prospect of meeting every need of every student seems overwhelming. When viewed through the lens of multiple labels for exceptionalities, cultural and gender differences, particularities of learning style, and intelligence preference, the impossible becomes terrifying—or else we dismiss as folly the notion that we could even know so many things about our students' profiles, let alone know what to do about them.

Differentiation does not ask classroom teachers to be specialists in dozens of areas. Rather, this way of thinking about the classroom encourages teachers to continually develop reasoned and reasonable approaches that will be helpful in working as effectively and efficiently with more and more students over the span of our careers.

One way of meeting that challenge is a sort of "anticipatory" planning. Most of us as teachers begin to see patterns emerge in our classrooms as our careers progress. For example, some students will inevitably need support with reading, which holds true in all grades. Some students will inevitably need additional work with vocabulary. Some students will work too slowly (for our preferences) and others too fast (for our plans). Some students will be significantly ahead of the others in knowledge, understanding, and skill. Some students will have trouble sitting still and attending for long periods of time. Some students will like word problems, and some will be terrified of them.

Our goal as teachers is to promote student success with essential knowledge, understanding, and skills. Learning problems inhibit student success. Student strengths are springboards for success. Perhaps a logical and manageable way to think about responsive instruction is to reflect on the student patterns we see and ask, "How might I plan to address key patterns in student learning as part of my classroom routines?" That sort of "clustering" of student needs seems more attainable than a misconceived notion of differentiation as an Individualized Education Program for every learner.

This clustering approach works much like what architects refer to as *universal design*. In the period after federal law began to require access to public places for people with handicapping conditions that make access difficult, architects discovered two important principles. First, it is easier and more economical to plan access as a building or structure is built rather than to retrofit an existing structure. Second, when they provided access-supporting devices for a particular group of people, many other people benefited from those devices. For example, architects learned that they could design and build a ramplike area into a sidewalk with far greater ease when the sidewalk was initially poured than if they had to rip up a sidewalk to install it. Furthermore, they discovered that although they thought they were building the ramps for people in wheelchairs, the ramps were also useful to mothers with babies in strollers, people with rolling suitcases, merchants with carts of goods, and so on.

Thinking about differentiation as a kind of universal design makes it seem achievable. In other words, if we began by asking, "What barriers to learning and what springboards to learning are predictable in my classes?" and then "How might I address those barriers and springboards as I plan the flow of my unit and lessons?" we would no doubt find the number of patterns more manageable than the number of labels and individual traits that surround us. Undoubtedly, if we also thought in terms of addressing the patterns as part of classroom routines rather than as interruptions to classroom routines, we'd be more successful in addressing them. Finally, it's almost certain that a "ramp" we think we are building for one student or one group of students would be of great help to others as well. Figure 6.3 provides a few of many possible illustrations of how a focus on patterns of student need and strength might benefit many students for a variety of reasons.

Selecting Instructional Strategies That Support Responsive Teaching

Another aspect of instructional planning for teachers in a differentiated classroom is selection of instructional strategies that lend themselves to addressing readiness, interest, and learning profile. Just as particular instructional strategies support teacher roles of presenter, facilitator, and coach (Figure 6.1), some instructional strategies are particularly well suited to addressing variance in student proficiencies with an idea or skill, some to responding to students' interests, and others to differentiating for efficiency of learning. Developing a repertoire of such instructional approaches helps teachers respond to academic variance in the context of promoting student success with essential learning goals.

Once again, thinking about *categories* of student need and instructional strategies for addressing them makes planning in response to learner need more manageable than the premise of planning separately for each learner. Knowing that I will have students who work at a range of readiness levels, for example, I will plan to use strategies such as tiering[2] or small-group instruction at points in the instructional cycle where misunderstandings

FIGURE 6.3
Addressing Patterns of Student Needs to Benefit Many Learners

Some Common Student Patterns	Sample Ways to Address the Patterns	Students Who Might Benefit from at Least One of the Sample Approaches
Need for reading support	Allowing option of reading partners/buddies when introducing new text Using a highlighter to mark essential passages in text and making marked texts readily available Systematically using teacher read-alouds to explore complex passages of text Providing excerpts of readings on tape	Students with learning disabilities Students learning English Students with low reading skills Students with auditory preferences Students who prefer learning with a peer Students with attention problems Students who have difficulty reading nonfiction material
Need for vocabulary building	Providing key vocabulary lists with clear explanations (vs. definitions) Pinpointing essential vocabulary (vs. long lists) Having students hunt for key vocabulary in editorial cartoons, on TV, in comics, in pleasure reading, in songs, and so on Using word walls or vocabulary posters with words and icons	English language learners Students for whom vocabulary and spelling patterns are difficult Students who have not had rich vocabulary at home Visual learners Students who benefit from contextual application of words Students with cognitive processing problems Students with attention problems

(Figure continued on next page)

FIGURE 6.3

**Addressing Patterns of Student Needs to
Benefit Many Learners** *(continued)*

Some Common Student Patterns	Sample Ways to Address the Patterns	Students Who Might Benefit from at Least One of the Sample Approaches
Difficulty attending in class	Using Think-Pair-Share groups Providing choices of tasks or modes of working Using multiple modes of teacher presentation Shifting activities during a class period Using graphic organizers designed to match the flow of ideas	Students with learning disabilities Students who enjoy variety Students at different readiness levels Students with varied learning preferences Students with attention deficit disorder or hyperactivity
Need to address strengths in an area of study	Using Jigsaw, interest groups, interest centers, or expert groups Providing advanced materials Encouraging independent studies Using learning contracts or learning agendas to personalize content	Students identified as gifted Students who find a disconnect between school and their interests Students with a keen interest in the topic Students who need/want to spend more time on a topic Students who like to share what they learn with others Students for whom choice is a motivator

FIGURE 6.3
Addressing Patterns of Student Needs to
Benefit Many Learners *(continued)*

Some Common Student Patterns	Sample Ways to Address the Patterns	Students Who Might Benefit from at Least One of the Sample Approaches
Need for targeted instruction and practice	Routinely meeting with students in small groups Assigning homework targeted to student need at key points	Students who struggle to learn Students advanced in learning English language learners Students who learn best in small-group settings Students with extended absences

often occur, where skills deficits emerge, or where some students are likely to have a need to work at more advanced levels of challenge. Knowing that students will bring different interests with them to school and that I am a wise teacher if I link those interests to the enduring understandings in the curriculum, I will elect to use strategies such as interest centers or specialty groups at points when the connections can be made to benefit student success. Similarly, because I know efficiency of learning improves when students can learn in ways that work for them, I'll build in instructional approaches such as visual organizers or intelligence preference options.

Some instructional strategies are effective in addressing more than one category of learner need. For example, RAFT assignments[3] are well suited to addressing readiness, interest, and learning profile simultaneously. Other strategies are easily adapted to respond to more than one category of student need. For example, an "expert group" is typically interest centered. However, a teacher can provide or recommend resource materials for expert groups in a way that attends to readiness needs as well. Figure 6.4 illustrates the idea of selecting instructional strategies to address categories of learner need.

FIGURE 6.4

Selecting Instructional Strategies That Respond to Learner Need

Category of Student Need	Some Instructional Strategies Effective in Responding to the Need	
Readiness	Tiering	Small-group instruction
	Compacting	Personalized spelling and vocabulary
	Think-alouds	Learning contracts
	Varied homework	Learning menus
	Highlighted texts	Materials at varied reading levels
	Text digests	Word walls
	Writing frames	Guided peer critiques
Interest	Interest centers	Independent studies
	Interest groups	Orbitals
	Expert groups	Independent studies
	WebQuests	I-Search
	Web inquiries	Design-a-Day
	Group investigation	Personalized criteria for success
Learning profile	Visual organizers	Intelligence preference tasks (Sternberg)
	Icons	Intelligence preference tasks (Gardner)
	Varied work options	Opportunities for movement
	Entry points	Varying modes of teacher presentation
Multiple categories	RAFTs	Complex instruction
	Graphic organizers	Personal agendas
	ThinkDots	Cubing

Whatever instructional strategies a teacher elects to use in response to learner variance should be used to help students understand big ideas, master essential skills, and work at high levels of thought on authentic tasks, with full knowledge of what will constitute success with the work. A goal of differentiated instruction is providing opportunity and support for the success of far more students than is possible in one-size-fits-all approaches to teaching and learning.

Asking Important Management Questions to Allow Instructional Flexibility

In addition to using classroom elements flexibly to support student success, clustering learner needs to make instructional planning more efficient, and selecting instructional strategies for responsive teaching, teachers in differentiated classrooms must think about management routines that support flexible teaching. Without such routines, it becomes quite difficult—if not impossible—to teach in a responsive or differentiated manner.

In a differentiated classroom, sometimes the teacher must work with one group of students while others work independently. Sometimes the teacher must distribute and collect more than one set of materials. Sometimes the teacher must give assignments for more than one task taking place in the classroom simultaneously—and so on. Although a differentiated classroom should support the sort of movement that comes with student-centeredness, it cannot support disorder.

In fact, the same sort of order necessary for effective and efficient use of student-specific attention is also necessary for a classroom that supports student meaning making. An important research finding is that "teachers who established 'orderly and enabling' learning environments were most likely to teach for meaning and understanding" (Knapp et al., 1992, p. 13). Thus, asking the right questions about and finding useful answers to management-related responsibilities of the teacher have a dual benefit in classrooms that support both the meaning-making goals of UbD and the intent of DI to ensure that meaning making is supported for the spectrum of learners. Figure 6.5 provides some categories useful in planning classroom management to support flexible and responsive teaching, poses some important questions a teacher might consider related to those categories, and provides a few illustrations of how a teacher might address the questions in practice. Chapter 9 will more fully illustrate how a classroom might proceed when a teacher plans with the principles of both UbD and DI in mind. The examples demonstrate how backward design creates a framework of high expectations for students and differentiation supports a variety of students in meeting those expectations.

FIGURE 6.5

**Some Questions and Answers Related to Managing
a Differentiated Classroom**

Some Areas of Concern in Managing a Differentiated Classroom	Some Useful Questions to Consider About the Areas of Concern	Sample Strategies for Addressing the Concerns
Managing time	How do I handle needs of varied students for more or less time to achieve goals?	Balance need for class to move ahead and individuals to move at own pace with homework, contracts, personal agendas, and so forth.
	What do I do when students finish work early?	Provide anchor activities and teach students to use them when they finish work.
	How do I find time to plan for differentiation?	Move slowly. Tackle one area at a time.
Controlling noise	How do I maintain an acceptable level of buzz in the classroom?	Provide and use signals for noise reduction. Teach students to monitor noise levels and adjust.
	What do I do about students who need quiet to work?	Use headsets or earplugs to block noise for these students.
Movement in the classroom	How do I move students among work groups smoothly?	Teach students to use task and team charts to locate where they should be and what they should be doing at a given time.
	How do I avoid having too many students moving around the room?	Designate one student in each group who may get up to get materials.
	What do I do about students who are distracted by movement?	Make a seating area in the room that faces away from the action.

FIGURE 6.5
Some Questions and Answers Related to Managing
a Differentiated Classroom *(continued)*

Some Areas of Concern in Managing a Differentiated Classroom	Some Useful Questions to Consider About the Areas of Concern	Sample Strategies for Addressing the Concerns
Flexible use of classroom space	How do I make the classroom flexible when the furniture is not?	Experiment with ways to rearrange furniture or to get it out of the way. Students can help you problem solve.
	How can I make best use of a classroom that needs to be larger?	Use centers-in-a-box. Have some students work on the floor when appropriate.
	How do I accommodate students who need to work alone?	Designate an independent working area in the class for these students, absentees who need to make up work, etc.
Organizing and distributing materials and resources	How do I get multiple materials distributed and collected smoothly?	Designate table or area materials monitors who fill this role according to your directions.
	How do I make sure different students get what they need to succeed with their work?	Use in-class personal folders marked with student name, class period, and seating area. Also helps keep ongoing work from getting lost.

(Figure continued on next page)

FIGURE 6.5

Some Questions and Answers Related to Managing a Differentiated Classroom *(continued)*

Some Areas of Concern in Managing a Differentiated Classroom	Some Useful Questions to Consider About the Areas of Concern	Sample Strategies for Addressing the Concerns
Monitoring student work	How do I know students' proficiency levels if they work with different tasks?	Develop a list of standards/criteria. Use copies of list with each student's name on a copy to spot-check work and record competencies and trouble areas.
	How do I learn about students from their work and my observations? How do I make what I learn useful?	Record observations on sticky notes as you work with small groups and individuals. Stick the notes in a notebook with a sheet for each student in alphabetical order (by period for secondary). Review them at least once a month.
	How do I keep track of who has finished what work?	Use student record keeping. Have students turn in assignments to designated trays or folders by task.

FIGURE 6.5

Some Questions and Answers Related to Managing a Differentiated Classroom (continued)

Some Areas of Concern in Managing a Differentiated Classroom	Some Useful Questions to Consider About the Areas of Concern	Sample Strategies for Addressing the Concerns
Making time for the teacher to work with small groups	How do I preserve time to work with small groups when everyone needs my help?	Let students know when you are "off limits" and why. Establish "experts" who will answer student questions when you are teaching small groups.
	How do I find time to plan for small groups?	Use materials already available to you. Do less grading of daily work. Go slowly but deliberately in learning to differentiate.
	What do other students do while I work with small groups?	Use necessary practice, anchor tasks, personal agendas, centers, contracts, and other strategies that students use to learn routinely and independently.

Teachers who use classroom elements flexibly to support student learning, cluster student needs to make instructional planning efficient, select instructional strategies to support responsive teaching, and seek workable answers to management questions will find themselves increasingly able to address the varied needs of their learners. Developing instructional plans through these approaches to support maximum growth of all learners in achieving high-level curriculum goals is a design for teacher and student success.

A Final Thought

Many of us who teach were once students in classrooms that did not exhibit the kinds of flexibility and responsive teaching used in differentiated classrooms. That history means we lack visual models of how such classrooms function. It may also mean that many of us have created classrooms of our own that are less flexible than they need to be to support a full range of learners in succeeding with meaning-making, authentic, high-level curriculum.

When someone suggests, then, that we move toward more flexible instruction, the response is often driven by uncertainty. Common responses are "I don't have time to do all those extra things" and "I don't even know where to start."

Sara Lampe, a longtime teacher and colleague, reminds teachers that we can change many aspects of our professional lives for the better—just as we can change many aspects of our personal lives for the better—if we have the desire to do so. She uses the analogy of someone who decides to change eating and exercise habits to become healthier.

There are many reasons to keep the old habits, of course, but they are not as compelling in their benefits as changes would be. So the first step is to determine whether we have the will to do better.

If we do, the changes are awkward at first. There's no time in the day to go to the fitness center or to cook differently. It feels like an add-on. But Lampe reminds us that there should really be a principle of substitution at work, not one of addition. In other words, we shouldn't lie around and watch TV for an hour as we always have and then go to the gym. Rather, we should substitute the gym for the TV time. We shouldn't eat the pizza and then eat a healthy meal. We should substitute the latter for the former.

In time, if we persist, the new habits become at least tolerable, if not comfortable. We begin to feel some sense of accomplishment in hanging on, and when we see results we'd hoped for, we find a new energy to persist.

Ultimately, if we stay with the program, not only do we become healthier, but the new way of life is no longer new. It's just our way of life.

Few people suggest that it is easy to change habits, but many people demonstrate the possibility of doing so, one step at a time. Many illustrate the benefits to their lives of doing so.

It requires persistent intent for teachers to break old teaching habits and replace them with routines that are flexible enough to support the success of many kinds of learners. Few teachers suggest that it is easy to make such changes, but many demonstrate the benefits of doing so for their students— and for their own sense of professional self-efficacy.

Notes

1. As noted earlier, exceptions to this premise would be students with severe cognitive dysfunction requiring IEPs that deviate markedly and consistently from content goals for other learners.

2. *Tiering* is a readiness-based instructional approach in which all students work with the same essential knowledge, understanding, and skill, but at different levels of difficulty based on their current proficiency with the ideas and skills. Tiering enables a student to work both with critical content and at an appropriate challenge level.

3. A RAFT assignment asks a student to assume a particular **role,** for a specified **audience,** in a certain **format,** in regard to a **topic** that causes the student to think at a high level about an essential idea in a unit of study. By varying the RAFT elements, teachers can address differences in student readiness, interest, and learning profile.

7

TEACHING FOR UNDERSTANDING IN ACADEMICALLY DIVERSE CLASSROOMS

How does teaching for deep understanding differ from "coverage-oriented" instruction?

How should we "uncover" the content to develop and deepen student understanding of important ideas and processes?

What instructional approaches help students to make meaning for themselves?

What about those students who haven't mastered the basics?

Understanding must be earned. Whereas facts can be memorized and skills developed through drill and practice, coming to an understanding of "big ideas" requires students to construct meaning for themselves.

Consider the following abstract idea: "Correlation does not ensure causality." Although the teacher or textbook can proclaim it, few students will comprehend its meaning without some active intellectual work, guided by the teacher. For instance, this idea might be introduced through a provocation, such as "Researchers have found that 95 percent of all persons convicted of violent crimes in the United States drank cow's milk as infants or toddlers. Therefore, we can drastically reduce violent crime by banning the use of cow's milk for children under 5 years of age." Students would then be asked to react to the proposal, while the teacher "stirs the pot" through guiding questions (e.g., "Is there anything wrong with this example?" or "Could the same be said of drinking water?"). Then, the teacher might present additional examples of correlations—some of which illustrate causal relationships and others that do not—and guide students in analyzing, comparing, hypothesizing and concluding. Next, students might work in heterogeneous groups to come up with additional examples and nonexamples. This lesson might culminate in student-generated explanations of why correlation does not guarantee a causal relationship. To reinforce (and assess) their understanding, students might be asked to individually develop a "lesson" for teaching the idea to others (e.g., younger students, an absent peer, adults) using their own words, pictorial representations, analogies, and new cases.

As the example suggests, teaching for understanding demands particular roles for students and teachers alike. Students are obliged to think, question, apply ideas to new situations, rethink, and reflect. Teachers are expected to stimulate thought, show examples and counterexamples, ask probing questions, set up authentic applications, play devil's advocate, check for understanding, and require explanation and justification. In a differentiated classroom, teachers use multiple approaches and support systems in these important roles to ensure understanding of a full range of learners. Teaching for understanding includes effective whole-class, small-group, and individual approaches. In the sections that follow, we will emphasize important principles and practices that enhance the likelihood that each learner understands the enduring ideas that define the content being studied.

"Uncovering" the Content

We frequently hear teachers refer to their work in terms of covering the content, often with the lament that there is too much material and not enough time. Their concerns are understandable given the pressures associated with content standards, accountability testing, and the widespread use of textbooks (with the unstated, but often felt, need to complete them before year's end). Nonetheless, we believe that the term *cover* conveys the wrong idea about the job of teaching. One connotation is to "cover up"—that is, to hide or obscure. Certainly *that* behavior is not our desire as teachers. Another connotation of the term is to "skim the surface" of the content that is to be taught. In this sense, we can "cover" more content by talking faster in class, but skimming the surface in this way is unsatisfactory if we value student engagement and meaningful learning.

When we seek to help each of our students come to an understanding of important yet abstract ideas and processes, we propose a shift in job description. Teaching for understanding calls for teachers to "uncover" the content. To examine this idea metaphorically, consider the image of an iceberg. A certain portion is visible above the surface of the water, but we cannot fully comprehend the iceberg without going below. Indeed, just as the bulk of the iceberg lies beneath the surface, the most powerful "big ideas" of content areas reside below the surface of basic facts and skills. When we speak of uncovering the content, we refer to teaching methods that go into depth to engage students in making meaning of content. A variety of methods—including problem-based learning, scientific experimentation, historical investigation, Socratic seminar, research projects, problem solving, concept attainment, simulations, debates, and producing authentic products and performances—have proven effective at provoking inquiry and engaging a range of students with content.

A detailed examination of each of these methods lies beyond the scope of this chapter, so we'll focus on three general instructional approaches designed to develop and deepen students' understanding of important ideas: essential questions, the six facets of understanding, and the WHERETO framework.

Using Essential Questions in Teaching

You will recall that we included essential questions in Stage 1 of backward design as a means of framing the big ideas that we want students to come to understand. Now in Stage 3, we use these questions to bring subject matter to life through our teaching. Consider the following essential question about content: If the content we study represents the "answers," then what were the questions? Not surprisingly, young people rarely have epistemological awareness (i.e., an understanding of how knowledge has developed over time and is validated within various disciplines). They tend to think of content knowledge as something that was just "always there" and that they must learn. One means of "uncovering" content, therefore, is to frame the content as the answers to questions or the solutions to problems. This approach provides learners with a glimpse into the origin and meaning of the content they are learning in a qualitatively different way than does a surface coverage of sterile facts.

For instance, in a course on U.S. government, students would be expected to learn about the three branches of government. Instead of presenting this information as dry content for memorization, consider introducing the content via questions such as the following: What might happen if people become too powerful? How might a country (or state) keep government leaders from abusing their power? Are there ways that power can be controlled? Questions of this sort are meant to stimulate student thinking about the *reasons* for the content, leading to a deeper understanding of its import. In this case, we want students to comprehend the need for a distributed system of checks and balances for controlling power, because unchecked power may lead to abuse of power.

Such questions are open-ended. Rather than leading to a prescribed "correct" answer, they serve as launching pads for exploring the larger ideas of power, abuse, need for control, and checks and balances. As students come to understand these concepts, they are more likely to appreciate the various "answers" found in the United States (e.g., three branches of government, two Houses of Congress, transparency in accounting, and a free press). Likewise, they are conceptually prepared to consider alternative approaches adopted by other nations, while being more sensitive to the abuses of power evident in more autocratic regimes.

Let's consider two more examples of essential questions, this time from the language arts, in which instruction focuses largely on skills and processes: How does what you read influence how you read? How do effective writers hook and hold their readers? The first question suggests a big idea in reading—that the way you read is influenced by the type of text you are reading. This question opens the door to a host of important reading concepts and skills, including reading genres, text structures, and various reading comprehension strategies matched to purpose and text.

In a similar fashion, the second essential question (How do effective writers hook and hold their readers?) serves to uncover a variety of writing concepts and techniques, including authors' style, voice, genre, organizational structures, idea development, audience consideration, and various types of "hooks." Instead of beginning with decontextualized skill drills and worksheets for reading and writing (which students often perceive as busywork), we introduce such questions to give learners a sense of the larger purposes of reading and writing. We might teach the five-paragraph essay format, but in the context of understandings about the importance of text structure and organization of ideas.

Teaching for understanding in skill- and process-oriented subjects such as the language arts and math cultivates a metacognitive awareness of *how* and *why* specific skills are beneficial and *when* they are best applied. Failure to teach skills in this way often results in mechanistic learning that fails to transfer (e.g., the student who "knows" the algorithm and can "plug in" the numbers into a decontextualized equation but cannot apply the very same skill within a more authentic word problem).

Essential questions serve as doorways to understanding. Such essential questions exist in every discipline and can be used to frame both content and process. Here are a few more examples from various subject areas (McTighe & Wiggins, 2004, pp. 89–90):

Arithmetic (numeration)
- What is a number? Why do we have numbers? What if we didn't have numbers?
- Can everything be quantified?

Arts (visual and performing)
- Where do artists get their ideas?
- How does art reflect, as well as shape, culture?

Culinary Arts
- When is it OK to deviate from the recipe?
- What makes a "safe" kitchen?

Dance
- *How* and *what* can we communicate through the "language" of dance?
- In what ways can motion evoke emotion?

Economics
- What determines value?
- Can macroeconomics inform microeconomics (and vice versa)?

Foreign Language
- What distinguishes a fluent foreigner from a native speaker?
- What can we learn about our own language and culture from studying another?

Geography
- What makes places unique and different?
- How does *where* we live influence *how* we live?

Government
- Who should decide?
- How should we balance the rights of individuals with the common good?

Health
- What is "healthful" living?
- How can a diet and exercise regimen be healthy for one person and not another?

History
- Whose "story" is it?
- What can we learn from the past?

Literature
- What makes a "great" book?
- Can fiction reveal "truth"? Should a story teach you something?

Mathematics
- When is the "correct" answer not the best solution?
- What are the limits of mathematical representation and modeling?

Music
- How are sounds and silence organized in various musical forms?
- If practice makes perfect, then what makes "perfect" practice?

Physical Education and Athletics
- Who is a "winner"?
- Is pain necessary for progress in athletics? ("No pain, no gain." Do you agree?)

Reading and Language Arts
- What makes a great story?
- How do you read "between the lines"?

Science
- To what extent are science and common sense related?
- How are "form" and "function" related in the natural world?

Technology
- In what ways can technology enhance expression and communication? In what ways might technology hinder it?
- What are the pros and cons of technological progress?

Writing
- What is a "complete" thought?
- Why do we punctuate? What if we didn't have punctuation marks?

Essential questions such as these are recursive in nature; that is, we don't just ask them once. They are used to frame larger ideas and processes and thus are meant to be revisited. Indeed, as students deepen their understanding over time, we expect more sophisticated and supported answers.

Such questions are also respectful of students' differences in prior knowledge, skill levels, and preferred thinking styles. The open-ended nature of essential questions invites *all* learners to think and respond. Furthermore, such questions can be easily framed to relate to students' varied cultures and life experiences. For instance, the questions "What happens when people become too powerful?" "When is the correct answer not the best answer?" "Where do artists get their ideas?" and "What makes a place unique?" can relate to lives of all sorts of learners and help them build a bridge between their own worlds and the content we want them to uncover.

Teachers who regularly use essential questions often note that the line between teaching and assessing becomes blurred. In fact, a straightforward and practical strategy is to pose an essential question at the beginning of instruction for diagnostic purposes. Initial student responses reveal what students know (or think they know) about the topic at hand, while exposing misconceptions that need to be targeted. The same question can be posed midway through a unit of study (as a formative assessment) and at the end of instruction, enabling the teacher (and the students) and to mark conceptual growth over time.

We conclude this section with six practical tips for using essential questions in your teaching.

- Less is more. A truly essential question can go a long way. We suggest employing a small number of essential questions per unit (two to five).

When using more than one, sequence the questions so they "naturally" lead from one to another.

• Be sure students understand key vocabulary necessary to explore the questions.

• Because the intent is to engage the learners, use "kid language" as needed to make them more accessible. Edit the questions to make them as engaging and provocative as possible for the age group.

• Help students personalize the questions. Have them share examples, personal stories, and hunches. Encourage them to bring in clippings and artifacts to help make the questions come alive.

• Post the essential questions in the classroom. Making them visible signals their importance and leads readily to teachable moments.

• Use follow-up strategies such as those in Figure 7.1 to engage far more students and deepen their understanding and their thinking.

FIGURE 7.1
Follow-up Strategies to Deepen Student Thinking

• **Remember "Wait Time I and II."**
Provide at least five seconds of thinking time after a question *and* after a response.

• **Call on students randomly.**
Avoid the pattern of calling only on those students with raised hands.

• **Use probes and follow-ups.**
"Why?" "Can you explain?" "Do you agree?" "How do you know?" "Please give an example."

• **Cue responses to open-ended questions.**
"There is not a single correct answer to this question. I want you to consider alternatives."

• **Ask students to "unpack their thinking."**
"Describe how you arrived at your answer."

• **Periodically ask for summaries.**
"Could you please summarize the key points of _____ [the text, the speaker, the film, our discussion] thus far?"

• **Play devil's advocate.**
Require students to defend their reasoning against different points of view.

(Figure continued on next page)

FIGURE 7.1
Follow-up Strategies to Deepen Student Thinking (*continued*)

• **Survey the class.**
"How many people agree with _____ [this idea, the author's point of view, that conclu-sion]?"
• **Pose metacognitive/reflective questions.**
"How do you know what you know?" "How did you come to understand this?" "How might you show that you understand?"
• **Encourage student questioning.**
Provide opportunities for students to generate their own questions.
• **Use think-pair-share.**
Allow individual thinking time and discussion with a partner, and then open up for class discussion.

The Six Facets as Instructional Tools

We briefly introduced the six facets of understanding in Chapter 3 and revis-ited them again when discussing assessment in Chapter 5. Now we consider the six facets as a framework for generating learning activities. Although originally conceived as a set of indicators of understanding, the facets have proven to be useful in generating ideas for "hooking" students around a topic, engaging them in higher-order thinking, causing them to consider other points of view, and prompting self-assessment and reflection.

Figure 7.2 presents a list of action verbs related to each of the facets. The verbs suggest the kinds of learning experiences that actively engage students in processing ideas and making meaning. Indeed, a number of teachers have reported that the facets have stimulated their own thinking about how to help students thoughtfully explore various topics. The graphic organizer in Figure 7.3, for example, shows the result of a brainstorming session by a teacher planning an introductory unit on nutrition.

The facets also play a helpful role in responsive teaching. When students display preferences and strengths in certain ways of thinking, the facets allow students to explore content in diverse ways. For instance, some teach-ers have students choose one or two facets to use in exploring a topic. After working with their facet or facets, they meet in a cooperative "jigsaw" group to share and hear from other students who worked with different facets.

FIGURE 7.2
Performance Verbs Based on the Six Facets of Understanding

Consider the following performance verbs when planning possible ways in which students may demonstrate their understanding.

explain	interpret	apply
demonstrate	analogies (create)	adapt
derive	critique	build
describe	document	create
design	evaluate	de-bug
exhibit	illustrate	decide
express	judge	design
induce	make meaning of	exhibit
instruct	make sense of	invent
justify	metaphors (provide)	perform
model	read between the lines	produce
predict	represent	propose
prove	tell a story of	solve
show	translate	test
synthesize		use
teach		

perspective	empathy	self-knowledge
analyze	assume role of	be aware of
argue	believe	realize
compare	be like	recognize
contrast	be open to	reflect
criticize	consider	self-assess
infer	imagine	
	relate	
	role-play	

Source: From *Understanding by Design Professional Development Workbook* (p. 161), by J. McTighe and G. Wiggins, 2004, Alexandria, VA: Association for Supervision and Curriculum Development. Copyright 2004 by the Association for Supervision and Curriculum Development. Reprinted with permission.

Such a strategy honors the recognition that learning is socially mediated (Vygotsky, 1978)—that we construct meaning and deepen our understanding when we discuss ideas with others, hear different points of view, and collaboratively "uncover" content.

Regardless of the approach, it is important to remember that the six facets are conceptual tools, not ends in themselves. The goal is *not* to try to come up with activities and assessments that use all of the facets all of the

FIGURE 7.3
Brainstorming Learning Activities Using the Six Facets

Use the six facets of understanding to generate possible learning activities to *hook, engage,* and *equip* students for desired performances and to *rethink* earlier ideas.

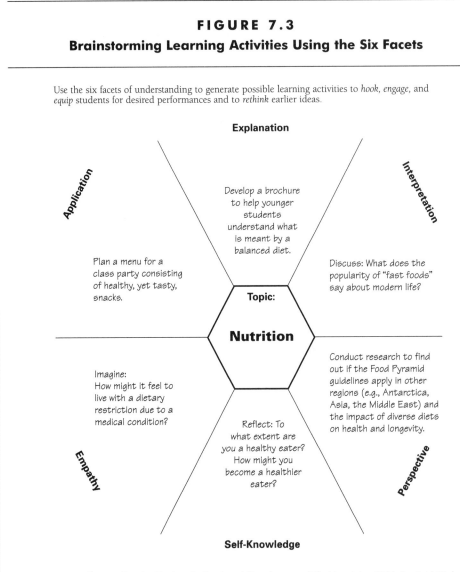

Source: From Understanding by Design Professional Development Workbook (p. 231), by J. McTighe and G. Wiggins, 2004, Alexandria, VA: Association for Supervision and Curriculum Development. Copyright 2004 by the Association for Supervision and Curriculum Development. Reprinted with permission.

time. Instead, one chooses those facets that will most meaningfully engage student thinking about particular content and serve as appropriate indicators of understanding that content.

A Reminder: The "Ladder" Is a Flawed Metaphor for Learning

When such "teaching for understanding" approaches are presented, it is not uncommon to hear teachers express the following concern: "Well, that may work well for the gifted, but I have students who have not yet mastered the basic facts or skills, so how can they possibly understand more abstract ideas or be expected to apply them?" Such worries are generally well intentioned, yet they reveal a common, but fundamentally flawed (in our opinion), conception of learning. This view may be characterized as the "climbing the ladder" model of cognition. Subscribers to this belief assume that students must learn the important facts *before* they can address the more abstract concepts of a subject. Similarly, they think that learners *must* master discrete skills before they can be expected to apply them in more integrated, complex, and authentic ways.

Two problems arise with this "ladder" view of cognition. It may make intuitive sense (as does the observation that the world appears flat), but it is at odds with contemporary views of the learning process. As cognitive psychologist and assessment expert Lori Shepard (Nickerson, 1989) notes:

> The notion that learning comes about by the accretion of little bits is outmoded learning theory. Current models of learning based on cognitive psychology contend that learners gain understanding when they construct their own knowledge and develop their own cognitive maps of the interconnections among facts and concepts. (pp. 5–6)

Just as toddlers do not wait to master the rules of grammar before they begin speaking, neither must any school-age learners fully master the fundamentals before attempting to use them.

Ironically, this belief about teaching and learning may have been unwittingly reinforced by Bloom's taxonomy, an educational model originally proposed nearly 50 years ago by Benjamin Bloom and his colleagues (Bloom, 1956). The irony lies in the fact that Bloom's taxonomy was never intended to serve as a model of learning or a guideline for instruction. Rather, it was developed as an assessment construct for categorizing degrees of cognitive complexity of assessment items on university exams. In addition, Bloom asserted the importance of all learners working at all levels of the taxonomy.

Nevertheless, many teachers over the years have used the taxonomy as a framework for a misguided approach to differentiating instruction—that is, higher-order thinking for gifted students and basic skills for lower achievers. *Using Bloom's taxonomy as a framework for differentiation is indefensible.*

The second problem with the ladder view of learning directly affects low-achieving students. Because they are less likely to have acquired the basics, struggling learners are often confined to an educational regimen of low-level, skill-drill activities, rote memorization of discrete facts, and mind-numbing test prep worksheets. The unfortunate reality is that many of these students will never get beyond the first rung of the ladder and therefore have minimal opportunities to actually use what they are learning in a meaningful fashion.

Recall the coaching analogy from the previous chapter. For too many students, much of their school experience involves the equivalent of decontextualized sideline drills, without the chance ever to play the game—that is, without the chance to engage in meaningful application of the content they study.

We are certainly not suggesting that the basics are unimportant. Instead, we believe that it is through the interplay of drill and practice in combination with authentic tasks (i.e., playing the game) that meaningful learning is achieved. Indeed, it is in the very attempt to apply knowledge and skills within a relevant context that the learner comes to appreciate the need for the basics. Thus, we caution teachers about withholding opportunities for the meaningful use of knowledge and skills from the novice or struggling learner.

Pulling It All Together: The WHERETO Framework

Planning precedes teaching. We propose that when teachers are developing a plan for learning, they consider a set of principles, embedded in the acronym WHERETO. These design elements provide the armature or blueprint for instructional planning in Stage 3 in support of our goal: teaching all students for understanding.

We have framed each of the WHERETO elements in the form of questions to consider. The design questions for each letter are posed to encourage the teacher to consider the perspective of the *learner*, who should always be at the heart of the teaching–learning process.

W = *How will I help learners know **what** they will be learning? **Why** this is worth learning? **What** evidence will show their learning? How their performance will be evaluated?*

Learners of all ages are more likely to put forth effort and meet with success when they understand the learning goals and see them as meaningful and personally relevant. The *W* in WHERETO reminds teachers to communicate the goals clearly and help students see their relevance. In addition, learners need to know the concomitant performance expectations and assessments through which they will demonstrate their learning so that they have clear learning targets and the basis for monitoring their progress toward them.

Consider the following example of the *W* in action: A middle school language arts teacher has a large bulletin board in her classroom on which she has affixed a full sized archery target (obtained from the physical education department). At the start of each major unit of study, she directs the students to the bulletin board and discusses the "target" for the unit—the major goals and the rationale for learning this content. As part of the unit introduction, she discusses the culminating performance task that students will complete during the unit. On the bulletin board, she has mounted a large version of the rubric (or rubrics) that she will use in judging student performance on the final task, and she reviews these criteria with the students. To augment their understanding of the rubric's criteria, she places examples of student work products collected from previous years (with student names removed) on the bulletin board. The work samples, which vary in quality, are placed around the target and linked to the different levels in the rubric. The samples provide tangible illustrations of the criteria and performance levels. There is thus no "mystery" regarding the performance expectations and the criteria by which student work will be judged. Not only does the bulletin board provide clear goals and the performance expectations at the start of the unit, but the teacher uses the student examples along with the criteria in the rubric to support her teaching and guide student learning and self-assessment throughout.

This bulletin board idea has been adapted for use by teachers of different subjects at various grade levels. By showing multiple examples that still meet quality criteria, teachers have found that they can allow differentiated products and performances without lowering standards. Multiple examples illustrate "diverse excellence" and help avoid cookie-cutter imitation by students.

H = *How will I **hook** and engage the learners? In what ways will I help them connect desired learning to their experiences and interests?*

There is wisdom in the old adage "Before you try to teach them, you've got to get their attention." The best teachers have always recognized the value of "hooking" learners through introductory activities that "itch" the mind and engage the heart in the learning process. Therefore, we encourage teachers to deliberately plan ways of hooking their learners to the topics they teach.

Here's an example: As part of a unit on map and globe skills, an elementary teacher begins a lesson on latitude and longitude by telling the students that they will be detectives and will solve the mystery of the Bermuda Triangle. After establishing basic information about the Triangle theory, she gives each cooperative group of four students a map of the region in which the Triangle has been outlined in dark marker. She then projects a list of coordinates where ships and airplanes have reportedly "disappeared" because of the Triangle's influence, and she asks the students to plot these points on their map. She provides a very brief demo of how to plot the points using latitude and longitude. The students quickly get the hang of it, and soon all of the points of missing crafts are recorded. The various groups then share and compare the plots on their map.

Guided by the teacher's questions, the class concludes that the Triangle theory is flawed, because many of the purported disappearances occurred outside the Triangle region.

The teacher then summarizes the activity by pointing out the latitude coordinates on other maps and globes and discusses their purpose. After the successful hooking activity, the teacher steps back and connects this learning to the larger goals of the unit and its essential question: "How do we know—and how do we show—where we are in the world?"

It is interesting to note that in this example, virtually no "stand and deliver" teaching occurred up front. The lesson did not begin with key vocabulary or readings from the textbook. Instead, the teacher hooked the learners with an interesting mystery and a challenge to solve it. By actively involving them in a purposeful and engaging use of latitude and longitude, she witnessed meaning making; that is, the kids saw the need for a coordinate system to locate points on a map or globe. By carefully orchestrating the makeup of the cooperative learning groups (including one high-achieving learner and one struggling learner), peer teaching became a natural part of the detective work.

Other examples of effective hooks include provocative essential questions, counterintuitive phenomena, controversial issues, authentic problems and challenges, emotional encounters, and humor. One must be mindful, of course, of not just coming up with interesting introductory activities that have no carry-over value. The intent is to match the hook with the content and the experiences of the learners—by design—as means of drawing them into a productive learning experience.

E = *How will I* **equip** *students to master identified standards and succeed with the targeted performances? What learning* **experiences** *will help develop and deepen understanding of important ideas?*

Understanding cannot be simply transferred like a load of freight from one mind to another. Coming to understand requires active intellectual engagement on the part of the learner. Therefore, instead of merely covering the content, effective educators "uncover" the most enduring ideas and processes in ways that engage students in constructing meaning for themselves. To this end, teachers select an appropriate balance of constructivist learning experiences, structured activities, and direct instruction for helping students acquire the desired knowledge, skill, and understanding (e.g., as displayed in Figure 6.1).

The logic of backward design becomes especially relevant in the first E of WHERETO. If we clearly identify desired results in Stage 1 and carefully consider the needed evidence in Stage 2, we can then plan backward to target the most relevant teaching and learning experiences (rather than just marching through the material from a textbook). In other words, our decisions about *what* to teach and *how* to teach in Stage 3 are guided by the priorities of the previous two stages.

When we target particular understandings in Stage 1 and plan corresponding performance assessments in Stage 2, we can readily determine what knowledge and skills those assessments require and teach accordingly. In essence, classroom instructors plan to equip students for their culminating performance task(s) in the same way that effective coaches prepare their team members for the upcoming game.

R = *How will I encourage the learners to* **rethink** *previous learning? How will I encourage ongoing* **revision** *and* **refinement***?*

Few learners develop a complete understanding of abstract ideas on the first encounter. Indeed, the phrase "come to an understanding" is suggestive of a process. Over time, learners develop and deepen their understanding by thinking and rethinking, examining ideas from a different point of view, exploring underlying assumptions, receiving feedback, and revising. Just as the quality of writing benefits from the iterative process of drafting and revising, so, too, do understandings become more mature. The *R* in WHERETO encourages teachers to explicitly include such opportunities.

For example, a high school photography teacher introduces the rule of thirds and has students take photographs that apply this compositional technique. After they have demonstrated an understanding of this basic rule of photographic composition, he shows them examples of stunning photos that break the rule for dramatic effect. In other words, the teacher deliberately challenges the one-dimensional idea that all compositions must follow a formulaic procedure to help the learners develop a more sophisticated understanding. Similarly, effective teachers of writing strive to move beyond the basic five-paragraph essay structure to explore the nuances of effective persuasive forms.

At this point, some readers may be thinking, "Yes, but this approach takes time. We couldn't possibly do this for everything we teach. So, when and how should we encourage rethinking and revision?"

We suggest that the *R* be considered when teachers work with *very important* content (i.e., enduring understanding) that proves difficult for students to grasp because it is counterintuitive (e.g., dividing fractions) or abstract (e.g., reading between the lines).

Over the years, teachers have used a variety of practical techniques to encourage rethinking and revision, including playing devil's advocate, presenting new information, conducting debates, establishing peer-response groups, and requiring regular self-assessment. As a reminder of the value of the *R* in WHERETO, we offer this maxim: *If it's worth understanding, it's worth rethinking. If it's worth doing, it's worth reflecting upon.*

E = *How will I promote students' self-**evaluation** and reflection?*

Capable and independent learners are distinguished by their capacity to set goals, self-assess their progress, and adjust as needed. Yet one of the most frequently overlooked aspects of the instructional process involves helping students develop the metacognitive skills of self-evaluation, self-regulation, and reflection. In their series of booklets on the topic, Art Costa and Bena Kallick (2000) caution that an education that fails to cultivate these "habits of mind" runs the risk of producing students who are incapable of thoughtfully and flexibly transferring their learning.

Teachers support these competencies by providing opportunities for learners to regularly self-assess and reflect on their learning. A natural way of promoting student self assessment and reflection is through asking questions such as the following:

What do you really understand about _____? What is still confusing?

How could you improve_____? What would you do differently next time?

What are you most proud of? What are you most disappointed in?

What are your strengths in _____ ? What are your deficiencies in _____ ?

How does your preferred learning style influence _____ ?

How does what you've learned connect to other learning?

How has what you've learned changed your thinking?

How will you make use of what you've learned?

Even teachers of primary grade children can begin to cultivate reflective learners. For example, a 1st grade teacher has developed a set of posters based on a cartoon frog character that signals the students (e.g., STOP and THINK: "How am I doing?" "Can I do this better?" "What have I learned?"). The posters are displayed throughout the room and serve as constant reminders of the importance of self-evaluation and reflection.

T = *How will I **tailor** the learning activities and my teaching to address the different readiness levels, learning profiles, and interests of my students?*

The *T* in WHERETO points to the importance of tailoring teaching so as to address differences in students' identified needs and strengths (i.e., readiness levels), interests, and preferred learning styles. Much of this book provides suggestions for such differentiated instruction.

O = *How will the learning experiences be* **organized** *to maximize engaging and effective learning? What sequence will work best for my students and this content?*

Finally, helping students achieve deep understanding of the big ideas calls for carefully organized learning experiences. The O in WHERETO simply reminds teachers to carefully consider the order or sequence of learning experiences as they decide the best means of reaching the desired results with the diverse group of learners they serve.

Traditional instruction typically follows a linear sequence (often dictated by the textbook) that builds from discrete facts and skills toward more abstract concepts and processes. Although such an approach may work in some circumstances, the wisdom of this climb-the-ladder model of learning is being challenged by experts, as we have previously noted.

Rather than having students master all of the basics before engaging in more authentic application, effective teachers immerse their students in meaningful and challenging tasks and problems (Stigler & Hiebert, 1999). Through contextualized grappling with ideas and processes, learners come to see the need for the basics as well as the larger purpose that they serve. Understanding develops and deepens by attempting to use knowledge in meaningful ways, not through decontextualized drill and practice.

For instance, consider the modern history teacher who begins his courses from the present and works backward to help learners see the relevance of the past in shaping current events. This thoughtful educator recognizes that the linear sequence of the traditional history textbook may, in fact, be at odds with the natural processes of learning. Similarly, other instructional approaches—such as problem-based learning, process writing, Socratic seminar, the 5 Es in science, and Web quests—reverse the conventional part-to-whole sequence in favor of more holistic experiences that require students to construct meaning for themselves.

In summary, the WHERETO principles embody research-based principles and reflect best practices of the most effective teachers. Therefore, the acronym serves as reminder for teachers to consider each element as they plan. Of course, it is not expected that each of the WHERETO elements would be seen within every lesson. Instead, WHERETO is intended to guide a *series* of lessons within a larger unit of study. We would, however, expect to see each element reflected within the scope of a comprehensive study of an important topic.

8

GRADING AND REPORTING ACHIEVEMENT

What are the nonnegotiable principles of effective grading?
What might reporting look like in a classroom shaped by UbD and DI?
What grading and reporting practices support learning and encourage learners?

For many teachers, grading is a conflicted exercise. On the one hand, they want to encourage and be advocates for the students they teach. On the other hand, teachers feel obligated to assume the role of judge and evaluator in order to meet the perceived dictates of the grade book and report card. These differing stances often seem contradictory, leaving student-centered educators feeling uncomfortable and compromised.

This apparent role dichotomy seems particularly confounding to teachers who implement responsive or differentiated teaching. Their classroom practice honors and attends to variance in student readiness, interest, and learning profile. In their classrooms, student variability is viewed not as a problem but as a natural and positive aspect of working with human beings. Seemingly in contrast, the report card and its surrounding mythology looms as a reminder that at the end of the day, students must be described through a standardized and quantitative procedure that appears insensitive to human differences. "I see how I can teach in a differentiated classroom," such teachers often say, "but how could I grade in one?" Yet, despite apparent contradictions between a standards-based education system and the need for responsive classrooms, we contend that sound grading and reporting practices can be a natural extension of a rich, differentiated curriculum and a seamless part of the instructional process.

Form Follows Function

Grading can be viewed as a two-part process: (1) assigning symbolic letters or numbers at the end of a specified time to serve as a summary statement about evaluations made of students' performances during that portion of the learning cycle, and (2) reporting the evaluation(s) to students and parents. We believe that the primary goal of grading and reporting is to *communicate to important audiences, such as students and parents, high-quality feedback to support the learning process and encourage learner success.* This purpose guides our thinking about how grading and reporting might look in a classroom, school, and district where backward design and differentiation guide educational practices. Translated into essential questions, we ask, "How will we know that we are providing high-quality feedback to parents and students? How might we ensure that the information we transmit in the grading and reporting process is useful in supporting the learning process? How should we grade and report in ways that encourage learner success?"

Guiding Principles of Effective Grading and Reporting

Like backward planning and differentiated instruction, grading and reporting are serious matters, requiring thoughtful consideration. Just as we recommended in Chapter 3 that content be organized around big ideas and organizing principles, we will anchor our recommendations for grading and reporting practices to six key principles.

Principle 1: Grades and Reports Should Be Based on Clearly Specified Learning Goals and Performance Standards

The logic of backward design dictates that we begin with a set of preestablished, clearly delineated, content-specific learning goals (Stage 1). We then determine the appropriate evidence of meeting those goals and select or design assessments to yield that evidence (Stage 2). Performance standards are then developed to answer questions such as "How good is good enough?" "What constitutes an A?" and so forth. Finally, grading and reporting provide the means of describing a learner's achievement level based on standards. As grading expert Ken O'Connor (2002) points out, "In order for grades to have any real meaning we must have more than simply a letter/number relationship; meaningful performance standards require that there be descriptions of the qualities in student work for each symbol in the grading scale."

In other words, a grade should represent a definable degree of proficiency related to important goals. Thus, educators should establish indicators of success, describe the criteria by which they will measure success, measure students accordingly, and report the results in a clear and consistent manner.

Principle 2: Evidence Used for Grading Should Be Valid

As discussed in Chapter 3, an assessment is valid if it permits valid inferences about desired results—that is, if it measures what we intend it to measure and not extraneous factors. If we want, for example, to measure a student's ability to apply the concepts of density and buoyancy, evidence of that ability should not be obfuscated by a student's limited English proficiency, learning disability, or inability to read directions. Grades should not be influenced by whether students forget to put their names on their papers or whether they have lovely penmanship. That is, insofar as possible, we need to eliminate factors and conditions that interfere with our students' capacity to demonstrate what they have come to know, understand, and be able to do. A grade should give as clear a measure as possible of the best a student can do, not be enshrouded in a fog created by tangential or constraining factors.

Principle 3: Grading Should Be Based on Established Criteria, Not on Arbitrary Norms

The meaning of a grade is compromised when it reports a student's achievement relative to others in the class. In such a norm-referenced system, a student might earn an A for being the "best" performer in a class of very low achievers or a C for being the "worst" student in a class of highly advanced learners. Furthermore, norm-based grading promotes unhealthy competition in which some students will necessarily become "winners" and others "losers" as they compete for scarce rewards (i.e., a limited number of As and Bs). We therefore strongly discourage the practice of grading on a curve (where it still occurs) and advocate a criterion-referenced approach in its stead. Rather than seeking a bell-shaped curve, we should be working toward a J curve—

a system in which all students have the possibility of earning high grades based on achievement judged against clearly defined standards.

In occasional instances where a student works toward learning goals different from those specified for others in the class (e.g., a student on an Individualized Education Program for learning difficulties or a student with an accelerated learning plan), the individual goals should be clearly specified. Then, appropriate measures—appropriate to those goals *and* to the unique circumstance of the learner—will provide the basis for grading.

Principle 4: Not Everything Should Be Included in Grades

Grading and *assessment* are not synonymous terms. *Assessment* focuses on gathering information about student achievement that can be used to make instructional decisions. *Grading* is an end-point judgment about student achievement. Whereas grading draws upon assessment data, it is unwise to mark or score all or even most assessments. For example, diagnostic assessments, or pre-assessments, should never be included in grades. They are conducted at the beginning point in an instructional cycle to determine students' proficiency levels, check for misconceptions, and reveal interests and learning profile preferences. They provide the teacher with valuable information to guide planning and teaching. It would be inappropriate to hold learners accountable for what they knew (or didn't know) *before* instruction. Formative assessments should rarely be factored into a final grade. These assessments give teachers and students ongoing feedback about the learning process, and they inform needed adjustments on the part of both. Formative assessments provide opportunities for students to practice, take mental risks, learn from mistakes, and revise their work. They enable teachers to analyze student performance to date and provide targeted feedback for improvement. This is not a time for heavy evaluation. (Of course, teachers may want to record information about whether learners have completed assignments, their willingness to revise deficient work, their persistence, and so on, for later reporting on students' work habits.)

Grades should be derived largely from the results of summative assessments carefully designed to allow students to demonstrate accumulated proficiency related to identified content goals.

Principle 5: Avoid Grading Based on (Mean) Averages

We join other grading experts in challenging the widespread practice of averaging all of the marks and scores during an entire marking period to arrive at a numerically based final grade. Consider the problem of averaging through the following humorous anecdote: A man is sitting on an old-fashioned room radiator that is blisteringly hot. His bare feet rest on a block of frigid ice. When asked about the room temperature, he replies, "On average, it's pretty comfortable!" This humorous story has a serious point: averages can mislead.

As an alternative to averaging *all* the marks, we strongly recommend that teachers evaluate students' achievements *later* in a learning cycle rather than including those earned earlier. If the goal is learning and a student accomplishes that goal in the eighth week of a marking period, the student should not be penalized for failure to demonstrate mastery in the second or fourth weeks. Second chances to learn matter more than speed of learning. Early scores are likely to underestimate a student's later achievement and to contribute to "grade fog"—a misleading picture of actual knowledge and skill levels. In other words, *what* a student learns should be more important than *when* he or she learns it.

O'Connor (2002) suggests that grades should be "determined" from various sources of evidence, rather than "calculated" in a purely quantitative manner. This process involves judgment. When our judgments are guided by clear goals, valid measures, and explicit performance standards, we can render fair and defensible judgments through grades. If averaging is required by the district, O'Connor recommends using the median or mode—not the mean—as the basis for arriving at a grade.

On a related note, we must comment on the practice of assigning zeroes to students who fail to turn in work on time or to complete assignments. The flaw with this tactic relates back to the fundamental purpose of grading: to accurately communicate achievement. If a grade is to provide a record of student learning of established content standards, then averaging in zeroes for missed work distorts the record. For example, a student may have learned the material well but be downgraded for missed work and actually appear (according to the grade) to be lower achieving than another student who completed all of the work but learned less.

The problem is exacerbated when a zero is factored in as part of an average. As grading authority Tom Guskey (2000) observes:

We certainly recognize the importance of students' work habits and believe that students should be expected to complete assignments, put forth effort, and follow reasonable guidelines. The point is to distinguish process from results. (By the way, one alternative to a "zero" is to assign an "I" for Incomplete or Insufficient Evidence followed by known consequences; e.g., staying in from recess or after school to complete required work.) (p. 48)

Principle 6: Focus on Achievement, and Report Other Factors Separately

A grade should give as clear a measure as possible of the best a student can do. Too often, grades reflect an unknown mixture of multiple factors. When other ingredients beyond achievement are included in a grade (e.g., effort, completing work on time, class participation, progress, attendance, homework, attitude, behavior, etc.), the problem becomes self-evident. Three students could earn the same grade for *very* different reasons. How effective is such a communication system? The problem transcends individual teachers. Unless teachers throughout a school or district completely agree on the elements and factor them into their grading in consistent ways, the meaning of grades will vary from classroom to classroom, school to school.

We acknowledge the importance of factors such as work habits in the learning process. Indeed, we recommend that information about work habits and other important elements be reported. Our point here is simply that these factors should be addressed and reported *separately* from actual learning based on established goals and performance standards.

Differentiation, Grading, and Motivation: A Special Concern

The six principles just described reflect a consensus of opinions by experts in assessment, grading, and reporting. These principles support the logic of backward design and a standards-based education system. Nonetheless, they raise a grading-related issue, especially in the minds of many teachers who differentiate their instruction. These teachers reflect a concern that grading can harm the motivation of some of their students.

In norm-based grading systems, struggling students are virtually doomed to live at the bottom of the grading heap. Learning disabilities, language issues, emotional matters, and other challenges generally persist in these students' lives. Thus, compared to students who do not have to work against those odds, struggling students will typically receive low grades year after year. It is a testament to human resilience that many students who struggle in school continue "the good fight" for weeks, months, and even years. Ultimately, however, it becomes apparent that no matter the effort they exert and no matter the growth they exhibit, the cards are stacked against them, and there is no grade-indicated evidence that their work results in success. After a time, such students are left to conclude that either they are stupid or school is stupid. Is it any wonder that those who invest in their schoolwork yet continue to harvest failure will arrive at the first conclusion? It is less damaging to one's sense of self to conclude that school is essentially flawed and not worth extensive effort.

In fact, either conclusion is costly in terms of motivation, achievement, and self-efficacy. To the degree that grades discourage struggling learners from putting forth the needed effort and investing in their own growth, there is a problem. This is certainly the case in differentiated classrooms where a sense of safety, appropriate challenge, mutual respect, and community are necessary hallmarks.

On the other end of the achievement continuum, competitive grading systems favor advanced students—often to their detriment as learners. These students are as destined to get high grades under such conditions as strugglers are doomed to get low ones. That scarcely seems a problem to most of us. How terrible can it be to be the beneficiary of guaranteed As?

In fact, competitive grading creates serious problems for advanced learners just as it does for strugglers. Such students learn early that effort is not a precursor to success. Ultimately, they begin to believe that if you are smart, you should not have to study. High grades begin to seem like an entitlement. Furthermore, our most able learners too often work only for the grade, with little regard for the benefits, the pleasures, and challenges of learning. Ironically, to realize their advanced potential as adults, these students will need at least three characteristics: (1) persistence in the face of difficulty, (2) the ability to take intellectual risks, and (3) pleasure in work. Competitive grading practices may unwittingly teach them exactly the opposite.

These concerns may seem moot given our previous recommendation that grades should be assigned in reference to clearly specified criteria and should not be based on a comparison with other students in the class.

However, there are two reasons for continuing the discussion. First, it is still the case in many classrooms that grades are issued in comparison to the peer group. Second, even if that were not the case and grades were reflective of performance against specified and worthy criteria, strugglers would still lag behind and advanced learners would be more likely to excel.

We believe that the heart of this problem lies in the grading system itself. If teachers are obligated to provide a *single* grade for a marking period, then they naturally consider a variety of variables, such as attendance, class participation, behavior, work completion, and attitude, along with achievement, when determining that one grade. This dilemma can be minimized or eliminated by reporting on several factors simultaneously.

Thus, it becomes necessary to examine the second part of the grading process: reporting.

Reporting Systems That Support Standards *and* Differentiation

In Chapter 5, we suggested that effective assessment resembles a photo album—a collection of evidence—rather than a single snapshot. In other words, a single measure should not be used as the sole basis for determining a student's achievement of important learning goals. As teachers, we are more likely to have a more accurate picture of what a student knows, understands, and can do if we examine multiple manifestations of the student's degree of understanding and proficiency.

Similarly, a single grade cannot effectively report all that we need to say about a student's learning. We join other advocates of grading and reporting reform in proposing that at least two, and preferably three, separate factors be reported: (1) grades for *achievement* of goals, (2) *progress* toward goals, and (3) *work habits*. We'll examine each more closely.

First, when the previously discussed approaches are enacted—agreed-on learning goals, valid measures of those goals, explicit performance standards, and consistent application of criterion-referenced evaluation—grades for student *achievement* will have greater clarity and meaning. Compared to a competitive, norm-referenced method, this approach allows a greater number of students the opportunity to "succeed" without lowering standards.

Second, a separate grade should reflect personal growth or *progress*. Since students come to each learning situation at different starting points and have varied strengths as learners, fairness demands an acknowledgment of where they have come based on where they began. When struggling students make significant progress along a specified continuum, that improvement should be reported and celebrated. Even if their overall performance level does not yet meet a criterion-referenced benchmark, their progress toward it needs validation.

Third, a more comprehensive reporting system will acknowledge productive *work habits*, such as completing work on time, asking questions for clarification, persisting when faced with challenging material, and listening to feedback and making needed revisions. Admittedly, these are process factors rather than results, yet they contribute to achievement and are valued both in school and in the wider world. Reporting on such habits acknowledges the hard worker while properly exposing the loafer. Of course, there is a need to agree on those habits we wish to include, operationally define them, identify observable indicators, and develop a continuum or rubric for assessment. In so doing, we act on a truism in school (and in life): What we report signals what we value. By including work habits in our reports, we signal that such habits are important and respected. By including habits as a separate reporting category, teachers can more honestly communicate about such matters as completing assignments *without* distorting a student's actual achievement in learning.

We advocate this multipart approach to grading and reporting on two counts: (1) clarity of communication and (2) impact on student motivation. The first point reflects the contention that a single grade should not be used to reflect multiple kinds of information. In other words, it is not appropriate to give students a single grade that "averages" or "blends" standards-referenced achievement, personal growth, and work habits. Such a grade obstructs our ability to provide clear, honest, and useful information to parents and students.

The second point is based on the realization that students are more willing to "play the school game" if they believe that they have a chance to be successful. If we limit success *exclusively* to standards-based achievement, we are unwittingly disenfranchising those students who work diligently and make significant personal gains, yet are hampered by disabilities, language, and other barriers.

We increase the number of learners who can have a chance at success in school when we base achievement on worthy criteria, chart each student's personal progress along a continuum that specifies those criteria, and provide each student's habits of learning as a part of reporting procedures. A far larger range of learners will likely persist with the enormous effort necessary for academic and intellectual growth. A struggling student might not yet show competence in some or all of the criteria specified for a grade level or marking period, but he could see growth and find encouragement in acknowledgment of effective habits of learning. A highly able student who can meet standards with minimal effort might better appreciate that personal growth is a more challenging and satisfying reward than is being celebrated for something he or she truly did not "earn." For both categories of students—and the many in between—a multifaceted grading and reporting system offers the potential to provide clear information about student achievement that can be used to support further learning and encourage student success. And success breeds success!

Reporting Systems

Thus far, we have argued for an expansion of the elements included in grades and reports. We conclude this chapter by pushing the envelope a bit to encourage educators to think in terms of "reporting systems" rather than just report cards. Reporting systems include multiple methods for communicating to parents and the learners themselves. Such a system might use report cards; checklists of essential skills; developmental continua for charting progress; rubrics for work habits; narratives; portfolios; parent conferences; student-involved conferences; or related means of communicating student achievement, progress, and habits. The richer the system, the more likely we are to achieve the goal of providing accurate information that supports future learning and encourages growth.

Individual teachers and schools are generally obligated to follow the grading and reporting policies set at the district level. Therefore, our recommendations call for systemic changes to the grading and reporting policies and practices in the majority of districts in North America. Some districts have already enacted such changes; others are planning to do so.

In schools and classrooms where reporting systems are not yet compatible with these recommendations, teachers still can report student standing relative to essential outcomes in a grade space, and attach comments reflecting progress and work habits. They can also meet with parents and students to explain and communicate the value of a learner's academic growth and approaches to learning. Such change aligns with our best understanding of the goals of teaching and learning.

A Final Thought

The principles of backward design, differentiation, and grading are not only compatible but mutually supportive. Figure 8.1 summarizes ways in which these principles and practices interrelate. Working together, they support our overall goal: clear, fair, and honest communication of standards-based achievement that concurrently honors the uniqueness of individuals.

FIGURE 8.1
Interrelationships Between Backward Design, Differentiation, and Grading

Key Principles of Understanding by Design	Key Principles of Differentiation	Key Principles of Grading
• Plan "backwards" with the end in mind. • Teach and assess for understanding of important ideas and processes.	• Differentiate instruction to address student readiness, interest, and learning profile.	• Use grades to communicate high-quality feedback to support the learning process and encourage learner success.

FIGURE 8.1

Interrelationships Between Backward Design, Differentiation, and Grading (*continued*)

Key Principles of Understanding by Design	Key Principles of Differentiation	Key Principles of Grading
Stage 1 • Identify desired learning results emphasizing big ideas and enduring understandings. • Frame the big ideas around provocative, essential questions.	• Target essential knowledge, understanding, and skill for all students. • Expect that all students work at high levels of thought and reasoning.	• Grade students in reference to clearly established goals and performance standards.
Stage 2 • Determine acceptable evidence of student learning. • Collect multiple sources of assessment evidence matched to the goals. • Look for evidence of understanding through one or more of the six facets.	• Pre-assess student readiness related to specified learning results to determine individual points of entry. • Use ongoing assessments to chart learner progress related to specified learning results and to plan instruction to support continued growth. • Allow students appropriate options for showing what they know.	• Align assessments tightly with desired learning results that are clear to teachers and students. • Base grades primarily on summative assessments that provide valid measures of targeted goals. • Determine grades based on clearly stated criteria, not on comparisons with other students.

(Figure continued on next page)

FIGURE 8.1

Interrelationships Between Backward Design, Differentiation, and Grading *(continued)*

Key Principles of Understanding by Design	Key Principles of Differentiation	Key Principles of Grading
Stage 3 • Align instruction with desired learning results and expected performances. • Include learning experiences that "uncover" the content and engage the learner in making meaning of the big ideas.	• Develop a learning environment that is safe and challenging for each student. • Focus student tasks clearly on enduring understandings and ask students to use essential knowledge and skills to achieve desired understandings. • Adjust instruction to address student readiness, interest, and learning profile, including small-group instruction, time variance for learning, exploring and expressing learning in a variety of modes, tasks at different degrees of difficulty, and varied teacher presentation approaches. • Work to eliminate factors that interfere with a student's capacity to demonstrate proficiencies.	• Provide practice and feedback to help students master desired outcomes. These should generally not be graded. • Report achievement, progress, and work habits separately.

9

BRINGING IT ALL TOGETHER: CURRICULUM AND INSTRUCTION THROUGH THE LENS OF UbD AND DI

How do the principles of backward design and differentiation look when they are used together in the planning process?

What are the potential benefits to learners of classrooms in which both models are used?

What should we expect to see in classrooms using backward design and differentiation?

To this point, we have examined key elements in backward design and differentiation, looked at support for the two models in theory and research, explored pedagogical connections between the models, and probed the issue of grading as it relates to backward design and differentiation. It's important now to offer a sample of how instructional planning might look for a teacher who uses backward design to craft curriculum and differentiation to ensure instructional fit for learners. That is the goal of this chapter.

A Quick Review of Essential Goals of UbD and DI

A brief summary of essential elements in backward design and differentiation is helpful at this point to focus thinking about the illustrations of how the two models work together that will follow in this chapter. Both Understanding by Design and Differentiated Instruction are complex and multifaceted to encompass the full range of factors a teacher must address in designing and implementing quality curriculum and instruction. The discussion that follows briefly describes essential elements in the two models as they would guide a teacher who embraces and integrates both models.

Teachers whose work is guided by the principles of backward design and differentiated instruction do the following:

1. *Identify desired learning results for the subject and topics they teach.*
   • Determine what students should know, understand, and be able to do as a result of the study.
   • Specify big ideas worthy of understanding.
   • Delineate enduring understandings on which the teacher and students will focus.
   • State provocative, essential questions that will guide students' exploration of the big ideas.
   • Articulate specific knowledge and skill that students will need for effective performance on the goals.

2. *Determine acceptable evidence of student learning.*
   • Decide what evidence will indicate that students understand the big ideas.
   • Consider what performances will indicate that the learners understand and can apply what they have learned, and by what criteria those performances will be judged.
   • Determine what will constitute evidence of student proficiency with the essential knowledge, understanding, and skill.

3. *Plan learning experiences and instruction based on the first two principles.*
   • Decide what essential knowledge, understanding, and skill needs to be taught and coached.
   • Determine how that should best be taught in light of the content goals.
   • Plan to ensure that learning is engaging and effective in the context of specified goals and needed evidence.

4. *Regard learner differences as inevitable, important, and valuable in teaching and learning.*
   • Persist in developing greater understanding of each student's readiness to succeed with designated content goals to enhance individual academic growth, interests that might connect with content goals to enhance motivation, and preferred modes of learning to enhance efficiency of learning.

• Work with students, family, and school personnel to understand and address learners' backgrounds and experiences, including gender, culture, language, race, and personal strengths, and to address those factors in teaching and learning plans.

5. *Address learners' affective needs as a means of supporting student success.*
   • Respond actively to students' need for affirmation, contribution, power, purpose, and challenge.
   • Understand and respond to the reality that these needs will be met differently for different students.
   • Understand and respond to the reality that a student's motivation to learn is tethered to a sense of affirmation, safety, and success.

6. *Periodically review and articulate clear learning goals that specify what students should know, understand, and be able to do as a result of each segment of learning.*
   • Ensure that each student has full access to essential knowledge, understanding, and skill in each segment of study.
   • Ensure that tasks and assessments focus tightly on knowledge, understanding, and skill designated as essential in a segment of study.
   • Ensure that all students reason and work at high levels.
   • Ensure that all students have equally engaging, equally interesting tasks.

7. *Use systematic pre-assessment and ongoing assessment aligned with designated goals to make instructional decisions and adaptations.*
   • Provide opportunities for students to build requisite competencies when assessment results indicate a student lacks precursor knowledge, understanding, or skill necessary for success with designated content goals.
   • Provide opportunities for additional instruction, coaching, or practice when assessment results indicate that need for a student or group of students.
   • Provide opportunities to advance or extend knowledge when assessment results indicate that a student or group of students has achieved mastery of designated content goals.

8. *Employ flexibility in instructional planning and classroom routines to support success for each learner.*

  • Use space, time, materials, student groupings, and modes of exploring and expressing learning flexibly to maximize the opportunity for success for a full range of learners when students work with tasks and assessments.

  • Use multiple modes of presentation, illustrations linked to a wide range of cultures and experiences, and various support systems to maximize the opportunity for a full range of learner success when students work with tasks and assessments.

  • Encourage each student to work at a level of complexity or degree of difficulty that is challenging for that student, and provide scaffolding necessary for the students to succeed at the new level of challenge.

9. *Gather evidence of student learning in a variety of formats.*

  • Provide varied options for demonstrating what students know, understand, and can do.

  • Ensure that students know what "success" looks like in their work—including both nonnegotiable class requirements and student- or teacher-specified goals for individuals.

Together, backward design and differentiation describe a comprehensive way of thinking about curriculum, assessment, and instruction, stemming from a shared understanding of what constitutes effective teaching and learning. In the instructional planning of teachers guided by backward design and differentiation, then, we should expect to see systematic attention to content goals they plan to teach and to the students who will learn them. In other words, such teachers will focus on clarity of goal and flexibility in arriving at the goal. Figure 9.1 illustrates how the big ideas of UbD and DI come together for classroom application.

We'll first take a look at a unit plan for 5th or 6th graders on nutrition. Notice how the backward design process is applied and how it contributes to goal clarity in all stages of the unit. Then we'll examine options for differentiating the unit. At that point, look for flexible approaches to helping a diverse group of learners reach the articulated goals.

FIGURE 9.1
Integrating and Applying the Big Ideas of UbD and DI

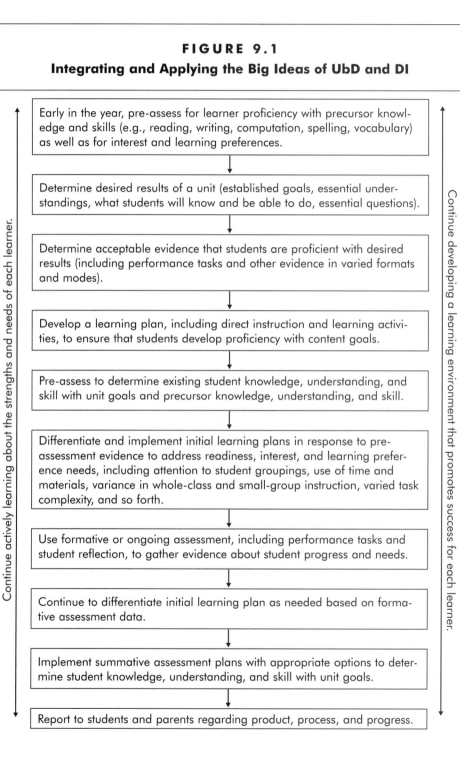

"You Are What You Eat": A Unit Planned with Backward Design

A group of upper elementary or middle school students will study the effect what they eat has on their health. The teacher who planned the unit drew upon content standards as well as a range of resources to engage his students in answering some essential questions about this important topic. What follows is the teacher's unit plan in a backward design format.

Unit Title: You Are What You Eat

Unit Focus: Nutrition—Health/PE upper elementary/middle school (5th–6th grades)

Topics: Nutrition, health, wellness

Summary: Students will learn about human nutritional needs, the food groups, nutritional benefits of various foods, USDA Food Pyramid guidelines, and health problems associated with poor nutrition. The unit begins with a personal survey of each student's eating habits. Throughout the unit students keep a chart of what they eat each day. They will gather information about healthful eating from various sources (USDA pamphlet, health textbook, video, and guest speaker), analyze a hypothetical family's diet and recommend ways to improve its nutritional value, and design an illustrated brochure to teach younger children about the importance of good nutrition for healthy living. In the culminating performance task, students develop and present a proposed menu for meals and snacks for an upcoming three-day Outdoor Education program that meet the USDA Food Pyramid guidelines.

Additional assessment evidence is gathered through three quizzes and a written prompt. The unit concludes with students evaluating their personal eating habits and creating a "healthful eating" action plan.

Print Materials Needed
• Health education textbook (chapter on nutrition)
• USDA pamphlet on the Food Pyramid

Internet Resource Links
http://home.excite.com/health/guides_and_directories/health_for_k_12/food/
http://vm.cfsan.fda.gov/label.html
http://ificinfo.health.org/infofsn.htm
http://www.nalusda.gov/fnic/educators.html
http://home.excite.com/health/diet_and_nutrition/diet_tools/quizzes_and_games/

Stage 1: Identify Desired Results

State: National Standard Number: Health 6

Title: McREL Standards Compendium

Descriptions

Standard 6: Students will understand essential concepts about nutrition and diet.

6.a: Students will use an understanding of nutrition to plan appropriate diets for themselves and others.

6.b: Students will understand their own eating patterns and ways in which these patterns may be improved.

Understandings

• A balanced diet contributes to physical and mental health. Poor nutrition leads to a variety of health problems.

(Related misconception: It doesn't matter what I eat.)

• Healthful eating requires an individual to act on available information about nutritious diets, even if it means breaking comfortable habits.

(Related misconception: If food is good for you, it must taste bad.)

• The USDA Food Pyramid presents relative guidelines for nutrition, but dietary requirements vary for individuals based on age, activity level, weight, and overall health.

(Related misconception: Everyone must follow the same prescription for good eating.)

Essential Questions

• What is healthful eating? To what extent are you a healthful eater?

• Could a healthy diet for one person be unhealthy for another?

• Why do so many people have health problems caused by poor nutrition despite all of the available information about healthful eating?

Knowledge and Skills

Knowledge: Students will know

• Key nutrition terms (*protein, fat, calorie, carbohydrate, cholesterol,* etc.).

• Types of foods in each food group and their nutritional values.

• USDA Food Pyramid guidelines.

• Variables influencing nutritional needs.

• Specific health problems caused by poor nutrition (e.g., diabetes, heart disease).

Skills: Students will be able to

• Read and interpret nutrition information on food labels.

• Analyze diets for nutritional value.

• Plan balanced diets for themselves and others.

• Develop a personal action plan for healthful eating.

Stage 2: Determine Acceptable Evidence

Performance Task 1: Family Meals

Topics: Nutrition, wellness, health

Summary

Family Meals: Students work in cooperative groups to evaluate the eating habits of a hypothetical family whose diet is not healthy (e.g., the Spratts) and make recommendations for a diet that will improve the nutritional value of their meals.

Print Materials Needed: Copies of sample diets that are unbalanced
Standard 6: Students will understand essential concepts about nutrition and diet.
6.a: Students will use an understanding of nutrition to plan appropriate diets for themselves and others.

Context of Use

This formative assessment is completed in class and is not graded. The student analyses of the diets and their recommendations will inform the teacher of potential misunderstandings that need to be addressed through instruction.

Performance Task 2: Nutrition Brochure

Topics: Nutrition, wellness, health

Summary

Nutrition Brochure: Students create an illustrated brochure to teach younger children about the importance of good nutrition for healthful living and the problems associated with poor eating. This task is completed individually and is evaluated with a criterion list.
Standard 6: Students will understand essential concepts about nutrition and diet.

Student Directions

Because our class has been learning about nutrition, the 2nd grade teachers have asked our help in teaching their students about good eating. Your task is to create an illustrated brochure to teach children in the 2nd grade about the importance of good nutrition for healthful living. Using cut-out pictures of food and original drawings, show the difference between a balanced diet and an unhealthy diet. Include pictures to show at least two health problems that can occur as a result of poor eating. Your brochure should contain accurate information about healthful eating, show at least two health problems that can occur as a result of poor eating, and be easy for the 2nd graders to follow.

Context of Use

This individual assessment task occurs approximately three weeks into the unit. The teacher can use student products to check for misconceptions. Evaluative criteria are identified to guide the teacher's judgment *and* the students' self-assessments.

Evaluative Criteria for Nutrition Brochure

The brochure . . .

• Contains completely accurate information about healthful eating.

• Shows a clear contrast between balanced and unbalanced diets.

• Shows at least two likely health problems associated with poor nutrition and explains the connection between diet and the health problems.

• Would be easy for a 2nd grader to follow.

• Is well crafted (i.e., neat and colorful).

Performance Task 3: Chow Down

Topics: Nutrition, wellness, health

Summary

Chow Down: For the culminating performance task, students develop a three-day menu for meals and snacks for an upcoming Outdoor Education camp experience. They write a letter to the camp director to explain why their menu should be selected because it is both healthy and tasty. This task is completed individually and is evaluated with a rubric.

Resources: Access to USDA Food Pyramid and Nutrition Facts for various foods

Standard 6: Students will understand essential concepts about nutrition and diet.

6.a: Students will use an understanding of nutrition to plan appropriate diets for themselves and others.

Student Directions

Because we have been learning about nutrition, the camp director at the Outdoor Education Center has asked us to propose a nutritionally balanced menu for our three-day trip to the center later this year. Using the USDA Food Pyramid guidelines and the Nutrition Facts on food labels, design a plan for three days, including the three main meals and three snacks (morning, afternoon, and campfire). Your goal: a healthy and tasty menu. In addition to creating your menu, prepare a letter to the director explaining how your menu meets the USDA nutritional guidelines. Include a chart showing a breakdown of the meals' fat, protein, carbohydrates, vitamins, minerals, and calories. Finally, explain how you have tried to make your menu tasty enough for your fellow students to want to eat the food.

Context of Use: Culminating assessment, evaluated using the analytic rubric in Figure 9.2.

FIGURE 9.2

Rubric for the Chow Down Performance Task

	Nutrition	Explanation	Conventions
4	• Menu plan fully meets USDA guidelines. • Nutritional values chart is accurate and complete.	• Highly effective explanation of the nutritional value and taste appeal of proposed menu. • Nutrition terms are used correctly.	• Correct grammar, spelling, and mechanics.
3	• Menu plan generally meets USDA guidelines. • Nutritional values chart is mostly accurate and complete.	• Generally effective explanation of the nutritional value and taste appeal of the proposed menu. • Nutrition terms are generally used correctly.	• Minor errors in grammar, spelling, or mechanics do not detract from understanding the overall menu plan.
2	• Portions of the menu plan do not meet USDA guidelines. • Nutritional values chart contains some errors or omissions.	• Explanation of the nutritional value and taste is incomplete or somewhat inaccurate. • Some nutrition terms are used incorrectly.	• Errors in grammar, spelling, or mechanics may interfere with understanding the menu plan.
1	• The menu plan does not meet USDA guidelines. • Nutritional values chart contains significant errors or omissions.	• Explanation of the nutritional value and taste is missing or highly inaccurate. • Many nutrition terms are used incorrectly.	• Major errors in grammar, spelling, or mechanics make it difficult to understand the menu plan.

Performance Task 4: Personal Eating Action Plan

Summary

Students prepare a personal action plan for healthful eating based on their unique characteristics (e.g., height, weight, activity level, etc.). The action plan includes nutrition goals and specific actions needed to achieve those goals (e.g., greater consumption of fruits and vegetables, reduced intake of candy). They are encouraged to share their action plans with their parent(s) or guardian(s).

Standard 6: Students will understand essential concepts about nutrition and diet. 6.b: Students will understand their own eating patterns and ways in which these patterns may be improved.

Student Directions

Information is useless unless it is used. Now that you have learned more about healthful eating, it is time to act on that knowledge. Your task is to prepare a personal action plan for healthful eating based on your unique characteristics (height, weight, activity level, etc.) and personal goals (e.g., to lose weight).

Include in the action plan (1) your specific goals related to nutrition and (2) the specific actions that you will take to achieve those goals (e.g., increase consumption of fruits and vegetables and reduce intake of candy). You should plan to present and discuss your completed Eating Action Plan with a parent, guardian, or other important adult in your life.

Context of Use: Culminating assessment, evaluated established criteria.

Other Assessment Evidence to Be Collected

- Selected-response/short-answer test/quiz.
  - Quiz 1: The food groups and the USDA Food Pyramid (matching format).
  - Quiz 2: Nutrition terms (multiple-choice format).
- *Prompt:* Describe two health problems that could arise as a result of poor nutrition, and explain what changes in eating could help to avoid them.
- *Observations:* Teacher observations of students during work on the performance tasks and in the cafeteria (while on cafeteria duty).
- *Student Self-Assessments*
  - Self- and peer assessment of the brochure.
  - Self-assessment of camp menu, Chow Down.
  - Comparison of their eating habits at the beginning with their healthful Eating Action Plan at the unit's end.

Stage 3: Develop the Learning Plan

Learning Activities

1. Begin with an entry question (e.g., "Can the foods you eat cause zits?") to hook students into considering the effects of nutrition on their lives.

2. Introduce the essential questions and discuss the culminating unit performance tasks (Chow Down and Personal Eating Action Plan).

3. Note: Key vocabulary terms are introduced as needed by the various learning activities and performance tasks. Students read and discuss relevant selections from the health textbook to support the learning activities and tasks. As an ongoing activity, students keep a chart of their daily eating and drinking for later review and evaluation.

4. Present a concept attainment lesson on the food groups. Then, have students practice categorizing pictures of foods accordingly.

5. Introduce the USDA Food Pyramid and identify foods in each group. Students work in groups to develop a poster of the Food Pyramid containing cut-out pictures of foods in each group. Display the posters in the classroom or hallway.

6. Give a quiz on the food groups and Food Pyramid (matching format).

7. Review and discuss the nutrition brochure from the USDA. Discussion question: Must everyone follow the same diet to be healthy?

8. Working in cooperative groups, students analyze a hypothetical family's diet (deliberately unbalanced) and make recommendations for improved nutrition. The teacher observes and coaches students as they work.

9. Have groups share their diet analyses and discuss as a class. (Note: The teacher collects and reviews the diet analyses to look for misunderstandings needing instructional attention.)

10. Each student designs an illustrated nutrition brochure to teach younger children about the importance of good nutrition for healthy living and the problems associated with poor eating. This activity is completed outside of class.

11. Students exchange brochures with members of their group for a peer assessment based on a criterion list. Allow students to make revisions based on feedback.

12. Show and discuss the video *Nutrition and You*. Discuss the health problems linked to poor eating.

13. Students listen to and question a guest speaker (nutritionist from the local hospital) about health problems caused by poor nutrition.

14. Students respond to the following written prompt: Describe two health problems that could arise as a result of poor nutrition, and explain what changes in eating could help to avoid them. (These are collected and graded by the teacher.)

15. The teacher models how to read and interpret food label information on nutritional values. Then, students practice using empty donated boxes, cans, and bottles.

16. Students work independently to develop the three-day camp menu. They evaluate and give feedback on the camp menu project. Students self- and peer-assess their projects using rubrics.

17. At the conclusion of the unit, students review their completed daily eating chart and self-assess the healthfulness of their eating. Have they noticed changes? Improvements? Do they notice changes in how they feel or look?

18. Students develop a Personal Eating Action Plan for healthful eating. These are saved and presented at upcoming student-involved parent conferences.

By using the backward design process, the teacher who developed this unit plan has established clarity about (1) what is essential for students to know, understand, and be able to do at the end of the unit; (2) what will constitute evidence that students know, understand, and can do those things; and (3) steps necessary to guide students to the desired outcomes. The teacher's clarity bodes well for student focus and achievement.

In most classrooms, however, student diversity is a powerful factor in how the learning journey progresses. That reality makes differentiation an important tool for student success—even in cases where teachers have designed carefully crafted, understanding-oriented curriculum.

Differentiating the Unit to Ensure Maximum Student Growth

Equipped with a clear and engaging unit plan, a teacher in a differentiated classroom would appear ready to guide students to success. Certainly the quality of the unit contributes greatly to the likelihood of success. Nevertheless, the class is likely to contain students whose skills lag behind grade level, students whose skills exceed the teacher's expectations, students whose interests vary greatly, and students who learn in different ways.

A teacher who understands that learner variability is also a factor in student success considers students as carefully as content and plans for their needs with equal care. The teacher typically begins a unit with a diagnostic assessment or pre-assessment designed to determine where students stand relative to desired learning goals.

In reviewing the pre-assessment data, the teacher saw the following:

• Four students already seemed to have a reasonably elaborate understanding of the targeted ideas and solid mastery of most of the key information and skills.

• Seven students had very little knowledge, and four displayed major misconceptions about key nutritional ideas.

• Six students could explain the unit understandings appropriately, but they lacked at least some of the key information specified as central.

• Nine students could explain the unit understandings in a very basic (but accurate) way and had some information about a few of the knowledge goals.

The teacher already knows that she has three students who are not proficient in English, two with diagnosed learning disabilities, two special education students on inclusion IEPs, one student with attention or emotional problems, and five students identified as gifted. She is also learning about the varied interests of her students and knows that they learn in different ways. Her goal is to use pre-assessment data along with other insights about her students to develop a basic differentiation plan for the unit. In addition, she will use a chain of ongoing assessment or formative assessment opportunities to adapt her instruction to the needs of varied learners as the unit progresses.

Whereas backward design ends with a stable yet flexible curriculum plan, differentiated instruction is, by definition, more fluid. Thus, a teacher's initial ideas about differentiation will evolve through a unit as students' proficiencies, misconceptions, and learning needs evolve. Nonetheless, the teacher can make some general plans for differentiation at the outset of the unit. Then, as the unit progresses, she can tailor the plans as necessary. What follows is a set of tentative plans from which a teacher might draw through the course of the unit. It is highly unlikely that any teacher would ever use all of these ideas in a single unit. However, having a broad repertoire of options for addressing learner needs makes it easier for a teacher to be appropriately and effectively responsive to varied learners. Among the options that a teacher may use are general procedures and supports that are broadly helpful across lessons and units, and adaptations specific to a particular task or product.

An Example of a Differentiated, Backward Design Unit in Action

When the time comes to move from curriculum planning to implementation of differentiated instruction, the last two stages of the backward design process must, of necessity, be reversed. In backward design, it makes sense to identify desired results, then determine acceptable evidence of those results, and then plan for teaching designed to ensure that each student succeeds with the desired results. In teaching (including differentiated teaching), it is necessary to proceed from considering where students begin the unit in relation to the desired results, then to implementing the teaching plan, and finally to gathering evidence of student success.

Following is an example of how a teacher might think about differentiating the nutrition unit as a whole. Each stage of planning suggested by the backward design process is included in the example, but you'll note that the stages flow in a "teaching fashion" rather than in a "planning fashion." Notice that the proportion of adaptations the teacher considers making to address the needs of varied students and support the success of each student in attaining the desired results reflects the proportions suggested in Figure 3.3. Very few modifications have been made in the "desired results" stage, many in the "teaching plan stage," and some in the "acceptable evidence" stage. Note also that the desired results serve as the rudder for most of what takes place during instruction and that the teacher uses differentiation as a means of ensuring that all students succeed with the desired results (and move beyond them when appropriate). In addition, you'll see that some adaptations are useful at both the teaching and gathering-evidence stages of instruction.

Focusing on Students in Relation to Desired Results

1. The teacher pre-assesses students to determine their entry levels related to the knowledge, understanding, and skills specified as essential for the unit.

2. The teacher gathers some information about student interests and learning preferences in ways that have direct application to the unit. As a result of the pre-assessment data, the teacher identifies and plans to address important precursor knowledge and skills with which some students will need help to achieve the desired results for the unit. These will become essentials for students who lack them—in addition to the knowledge and skills specified as essential for the unit. These students will also, of course, work with the unit's enduring understandings.

3. Also as a result of the pre-assessment, the teacher identifies some students who have already mastered skills and acquired knowledge she plans to teach in the unit. She will plan to provide these students with alternate work

when appropriate to ensure their continuing growth. They will also work with the unit's enduring understandings.

4. Two students have Individualized Education Programs that require attention to skills not included as essential for the unit. The teacher notes those as well and plans to address them in partnership with the special education teacher. Both of these students will also work with the unit's enduring understandings.

Carrying Out and Differentiating the Teaching Plan

1. When students are asked to read the health text, the teacher offers or provides supported reading for students who have difficulty with text material (e.g., reading buddies, taped portions of the text, highlighted texts, graphic organizers for distilling text, double entry journals, read-alouds, etc.).

2. When key vocabulary is introduced, the teacher provides key word lists with simple definitions and icons or illustrations for English language learners, inclusion students, and others who struggle with vocabulary.

3. The teacher ensures that students who do not speak English fluently have access to some means of bridging the student's first language and English. Such approaches might include student groupings that include a student who speaks both languages, dual-language dictionaries, Internet sites on the topic in the student's first language, opportunities to brainstorm in a first language before writing in a new language, or writing in the new language followed by conversation and editing in the student's first language.

4. The teacher provides or suggests resources at a range of reading levels and at varying degrees of content complexity so that all students have access to materials that are appropriately challenging for their needs.

5. The teacher uses small-group instruction to conduct the concept attainment lesson and categorization activity only with students for whom the pre-assessment indicates a need to establish the concept of food groups.

6. In class discussions and student discussion groups, the teacher makes certain to connect enduring understandings with a variety of student experiences, cultures, interests, and perspectives.

7. The teacher uses a variety of techniques such as Think-Pair-Share and random calling on students to ensure that everyone has the opportunity and expectation to contribute to class understanding. When appropriate for particular students, the teacher scaffolds student responses through techniques

such as cueing students about upcoming questions and asking students to build on one another's ideas.

8. On occasion, the teacher provides varied homework assignments when appropriate to ensure that student time is effectively used to address their particular needs.

9. When the speaker comes, the teacher asks a student who does not sit and listen well to be responsible for videotaping the session.

10. The teacher models how to read and interpret food labels briefly for the whole class and then offers a mini-workshop for students who want or need additional practice with the labels before beginning the related task.

11. The teacher makes consistent use of small-group instruction based on formative or ongoing assessment data to find alternate ways of teaching to clear up misconceptions for some students, demonstrate application of skills for some students, and extend the unit's challenge level for some students. Such groups are flexible in composition and reflect the fluid nature of learning in a classroom.

12. When ongoing or formative assessments indicate that a student has mastered particular skills, the teacher ensures that the student works with alternate assignments that are relevant, interesting, and challenging for those students.

13. The teacher invites students to propose alternate ways of accomplishing goals beyond those she provides to students.

14. The teacher uses "heads up" oral reminders to the class as she informally observes student work to call student attention to potential trouble spots in their tasks and responses.

15. The teacher uses regular "teacher talk" groups as one assessment strategy to help her get a sense of how students' work is progressing, where they are confused or "stuck," how they are using their time, and other factors that will enable her to assist them more effectively.

16. The teacher offers periodic miniworkshops (with specific students sometimes invited to attend) on skills or topics with which students may experience difficulty as they work or on skills or topics designed to push forward the thinking and production of advanced learners.

17. The teacher offers students the option of working alone or with a partner when feasible so that students may work in a way that's most comfortable and effective for them.

18. The teacher uses rubrics with elements and criteria focused on key content goals as well as personalized elements designed to appropriately challenge various learners and cause them to attend to particular facets of the work important to their own development. At this stage in instruction, she introduces the rubrics to students so that they are familiar with them and with their requirements when they begin work with their products or assessment tasks.

19. The teacher tiers activities when appropriate so that all students are working toward the same content goals but at different degrees of difficulty so that each student works at an appropriate challenge level.

20. The teacher offers students varied modes of exploring or expressing learning when appropriate.

Determining Student Success

1. The teacher gives quizzes orally to students who need to have questions read aloud. Students who need additional time to write answers take the quizzes in two parts (on two days).

2. The teacher continues to ensure that students who do not speak English fluently have access to some means of bridging their first language and English. Such a strategy might include student groupings that include a student who speaks both languages, dual-language dictionaries, Internet sites on the topic in the student's first language, opportunities to brainstorm in a first language before writing in a new language, or writing in the new language followed by conversation and editing in the student's first language.

3. The teacher provides or suggests resources at a range of reading levels and at varying degrees of content complexity so that all students have access to materials that are appropriately challenging for their needs.

4. The teacher invites students to propose alternate ways of accomplishing assessment goals beyond those she provides to students.

5. The teacher provides some options for varied ways to express the desired outcomes.

6. The teacher guides or directs the work of one or more small groups for students who need adult guidance periodically throughout their product or assessment work.

7. The teacher offers students the option of working alone or with a partner when appropriate so that students may work in a way that is most comfortable and effective for them.

8. The teacher uses rubrics with elements and criteria focused on key content goals as well as personalized elements designed to appropriately challenge various learners and cause them to attend to particular facets of the work important to their own development.

9. Students can request peer consultation directed by critique guides that focus the "consultant" on key product requirement delineated in rubrics.

10. The teacher provides optional planning templates or organizers to guide students' product or assessment work.

11. The teacher continues to use regular "teacher talk" groups as a means of helping her get a sense of how students' work is progressing, where they are confused or "stuck," how they are using their time, and other factors that will enable her to coach them more effectively.

It's important to reiterate that it is not our intent to suggest that any teacher would make *all* of these modifications in a given unit, but rather to illustrate many ways a teacher can adapt a high-quality curriculum plan to address the varied learning needs of students with the goal of maximizing the possibility of success for each student in achieving the unit's desired outcomes. Now it's useful to take a look at how a specific portion of the nutrition unit might be differentiated using some of the general approaches noted here—and some other approaches to differentiation as well.

An Example of a Specific Adjustment to an Assignment

In addition to drawing upon a range of more generic approaches to addressing a range of student readiness needs, a teacher can examine any task or assessment to determine whether some students might benefit from a differentiated version of the work and how the work might be modified to benefit particular learners. Following is a summary of one assessment task in the nutrition unit and differentiated versions of the task the teacher might develop in response to student readiness, interest, and learning profile needs. The adaptations reflect the kinds of needs revealed in the unit's pre-assessment and formative assessments. The example illustrates how a teacher can take a planned assessment and modify it to address varied readiness levels, particular student interests, and a range of learning profile preferences without departing from the unit's essential goals. Again, it is not the intent of the examples to suggest that a teacher should use all of the options but rather to show how differentiating even a well-constructed task might make it more effective for particular students.

The Original Activity (Not Differentiated)

Because our class has been learning about nutrition, 2nd grade teachers in our school have asked our help in teaching their students about good eating. Create an illustrated brochure to teach the 2nd graders about the importance of good nutrition for healthful living. Use cut-out pictures of food and original drawings to show the difference between a balanced diet and an unhealthy diet. Show at least two health problems that can occur as a result of poor eating. Your brochure should also contain accurate information and should be easy for 2nd graders to read and understand.

Differentiated Versions of the Activity

To address readiness needs

Students who are having difficulty with the basic principles of nutrition and the consequences of nutritional decisions, as well as with reading and writing, will complete the original version.

Students who have a basic understanding of principles of nutrition and their consequences will have a similar version that asks them to write their brochures for elementary students who are interested in becoming healthy middle schoolers. They will also be asked to present at least six essential nutritional guidelines for the elementary students in their brochure. Following these guidelines should make it more likely the students will become healthy middle schoolers. Rather than use cut-outs and drawings, students will be asked to develop icons that represent the key guidelines for good nutrition and help call attention to the meaning of the guideline that they represent.

Students who are very advanced in their knowledge and understanding of the vocabulary and principles of good nutrition and who are advanced readers will be asked to develop a brochure to be used in a pediatrician's office for young people between the ages of 10 and 16 who visit the office—and for the parents of these young people. The brochure should offer accurate and important information and guidance about nutritional decisions, doing so in ways likely to catch the attention of the audience and to be memorable to them rather than boring them or being a turn-off to the topic.

Students in the class who are *very* nutrition-savvy *and have a strong interest* in the topic will design a specialty brochure for distribution at a health center, aimed at adolescents and their parents who already pay a lot of attention to nutrition at home and who want to become more sophisticated in their decision making. Their brochure should be accurate and attractive, and also aimed at a knowledgeable audience.

To tap student interests

Students have the option to include in their brochures some nutritional information about specific roles or groups that they are interested in thinking about, as well as the nutritional needs of those groups. For example, specific nutritional guidance for runners, football players, teenagers, people with allergies or asthma, models, and pilots would enable students to move from more general information to particular needs and to see how information applies to varied individuals and groups. To assist with this aspect of the work, the teacher convenes groups of students with a similar interest focus to share ideas as they complete their brochures.

Students have the option of completing the task for students whose school is in a culture other than the United States and in which they have a particular interest (e.g., good nutrition in Mexico or Iraq).

To address student learning preferences

Students are given a choice of several ways that their knowledge, understanding, and skill might be demonstrated. For example, instead of having only the option of a brochure, students might be invited to complete the task in the form of annotated storyboards for a series of public service announcements, a three-part column in a magazine for students of a specified age, an essay on a Web site, or a position paper to be shared with the managers of a school cafeteria.

Students have the option of working alone or with a team on the *design* of their product, although they must ultimately complete the product alone.

All of these possible modifications—and many other options not described here—have two primary purposes: (1) to ensure maximum growth for the full range of learners in achieving important curricular outcomes and (2) to provide flexible yet valid evidence of student understanding. With success in mastering important ideas and skills comes a whole array of other benefits—among them a sense of self-efficacy, an appreciation of the power of knowledge, a realization of one's power as a learner, and a sense of belonging and contributing to a community of learners. Powerful curriculum is essential in effective classrooms—and so is the capacity to connect each learner to that curriculum in a way that succeeds for the learner. Backward design addresses the former and differentiation the latter. Both elements must work, and work in concert, for schools to effectively serve the full array of students entrusted to them.

Observable Indicators in UbD/DI Classrooms

What should we see when teachers have integrated the principles and practices of Understanding by Design and Differentiated Instruction into the fabric of their classrooms? This section lists a set of observable indicators, organized around four categories: "The Learning Environment," "The Curriculum," "The Teacher," and "The Learner" (adapted from McTighe & Seif, 2002). This list may seem daunting, but we would not expect to see every one of these indicators on every single visit to a classroom. Nonetheless, we believe that teachers who understand and embrace the key ideas of UbD and DI will naturally and consistently seek to integrate them into their repertoire. Over time, a growing number of such indicators will become the norm.

The Learning Environment

- Each student is treated with dignity and respect.
- Each student feels safe and valued in the classroom.
- Each student makes meaningful contributions to the work of the group.
- There is a balanced emphasis on individuals and the group as a whole.
- Students work together collaboratively.
- Students are grouped flexibly to ensure attention to both their similarities to and differences from peers.
- Evidence indicates that varied student perspectives are sought and various approaches to learning are honored.
- The big ideas and essential questions are central to the work of the students, the classroom activity, and the norms and culture of the classroom.
- There are high expectations and incentives for each student to learn the big ideas and answer the essential questions.
- All students have respectful work—that is, tasks and assessments focused on what matters most in the curriculum, tasks structured to

necessitate high-level thinking, and tasks that are equally appealing and engaging to learners.

- Big ideas, essential questions, and criteria/scoring rubrics are posted.
- Samples/models of student work are visible.

The Curriculum

- Units and courses reflect a coherent design; content standards, big ideas, and essential questions are clearly aligned with assessments and learning activities.
- There are multiple ways to take in and explore ideas.
- Multiple forms of assessment allow students to demonstrate their understanding in various ways.
- Assessment of understanding is anchored by "authentic" performance tasks calling for students to demonstrate their understanding through application and explanation.
- Teacher, peer, and self-evaluations of student products or performances include clear criteria and performance standards for the group as well as attention to individual needs and goals.
- The unit or course design enables students to revisit and rethink important ideas to deepen their understanding.
- The teacher and students use a variety of resources. The textbook is only one resource among many. Resources reflect different cultural backgrounds, reading levels, interests, and approaches to learning.

The Teacher

- The teacher informs students of the big ideas and essential questions, performance requirements, and evaluative criteria at the beginning of the unit or course and continues to reflect on those elements with students throughout the unit.
- The teacher helps students connect the big ideas and essential questions of the unit with their backgrounds, interests, and aspirations.
- The teacher hooks and holds students' interest while they examine and explore big ideas and essential questions. This approach includes acknowledging and building on the variety of student interests in the class.
- The teacher helps students establish and achieve personal learning goals in addition to important content goals for the class as a whole.

• The teacher uses a variety of instructional strategies and interacts with students in multiple ways to promote deeper understanding of subject matter for each student.

• The teacher uses information from pre-assessments and ongoing assessments to determine skills needs, check for understanding, uncover misconceptions, provide feedback for improvement, and make instructional modifications.

• The teacher routinely provides for student differences in readiness, interest, and mode of learning.

• The teacher facilitates students' active construction of meaning, rather than simply "telling." The teacher understands that individual learners will make meaning in different ways and on different timetables.

• The teacher uses a variety of strategies to support students' varying needs for growth in reading, writing, vocabulary, planning, and other fundamental skills that enable academic success.

• The teacher uses questioning, probing, and feedback to encourage learners to "unpack their thinking," reflect, and rethink.

• The teacher uses a variety of resources (more than only the textbook) to promote understanding.

• The teacher provides meaningful feedback to parents and students about students' achievement, progress, and work habits.

The Learners

• Students can describe the goals (big ideas and essential questions) and the performance requirements of the unit or course.

• Students can explain what they are doing and why (i.e., how today's work relates to the larger goals).

• Students can explain how their classroom functions and how its various elements work to support success of each learner and of the class as a whole.

• Students contribute actively to effective functioning of classroom routines and share responsibility with the teacher for making the class work.

• Students are hooked at the beginning and engaged throughout the unit as a result of the nature of the curriculum and the appropriateness of instruction for their particular learning needs.

- Students can describe both the group and individual criteria by which their work will be evaluated.
- Students are engaged in activities that help them learn the big ideas and answer the essential questions.
- All students have opportunities to generate relevant questions and share interests and perspectives.
- Students are able to explain and justify their work and their answers.
- Students are involved in self- or peer assessment based on established criteria and performance standards.
- Students use the criteria/rubric(s) to guide and revise their work.
- Students regularly reflect on and set goals related to their achievement, progress, and work habits.

A Final Thought

Understanding by Design is a sophisticated planning process. It demands in-depth content knowledge, the capacity to "think like an assessor," concern for authenticity in learning activities and assessments, explicit attention to student rethinking, a blending of facilitative and directed teaching, and the disposition to critically examine one's plans and adjust based on feedback and results. Differentiated Instruction is also a complex process. It demands continual attention to the strengths and needs of learners who not only change with the passage of each year but evolve during the school year as well. It requires the capacity to create flexible teaching–learning routines that enable academically diverse student populations to succeed with rich, challenging academic content and processes, and to create learning environments that are both supportive and challenging for students for whom those conditions will differ.

When integrated, the two frameworks certainly challenge teachers, but they also reflect the best of content- *and* learner-centered planning, teaching, and assessing. Both approaches require that teachers be willing to move out of their educational comfort zone, risk the initial uneasiness of expanding their repertoire, constantly reflect on the impact of their actions, and make adjustments for improvement. We believe the effort will pay off in more engaging and effective classrooms—for students and teachers alike. In the end, that's what makes teaching both dynamic and satisfying.

10

MOVING FORWARD TO INTEGRATE UbD AND DI

How should we act on the ideas in this book?

Former president Herbert Hoover once observed, "Words without actions are the assassins of idealism." We think that his idea applies to this book. Throughout the previous chapters, we have provided a rationale for linking Understanding by Design and Differentiated Instruction. We have examined principles and practices related to curriculum, instruction, assessment, grading, and reporting. We have described how a UbD curriculum unit can become more responsive to the varying needs of learners. Now we face the practical questions: How might we apply the ideas in this book? What should we do to more effectively link UbD and DI? What actions can we take to enhance responsive teaching of important content?

There is no single "best" way of integrating the ideas of these two frameworks. Indeed, many possibilities and pathways exist. In the spirit of this book, we suggest that you use the backward design process to help you plan an effective course of action. Here are some general considerations followed by specific actions.

Stage 1

Begin by considering the *desired results* you seek by connecting UbD and DI, whether as an individual teacher, a team or department leader, a school-based administrator, or a district-level staff person. Desired results for learners could include outcomes such as the following:

• Deeper understanding of "big ideas" within content standards by all students

• Greater interest and engagement in school among each student population

• Higher-quality student work for each student on tasks that are meaningful for each student

• Improved achievement for each population of learners

In addition to learner outcomes, desired results include advances that you would like to realize in your classroom, school, or district. For example, you may want to focus your teaching more overtly on exploring big ideas through essential questions. Maybe you desire to better connect the content with your students' interests. Maybe there is a need to implement more flexible instructional and management routines in classrooms. Perhaps you recognize a need to use diagnostic assessments to identify misconceptions and skill gaps or to use ongoing assessments as a means to modify instructional plans in ways that lead to greater success for more students. It may be time to redesign the district's grading policy and report card to incorporate the ideas presented in Chapter 8.

As you consider desired results for learners *and* educators, we recommend that you consider "data" (in the broad sense of the term). For example: What changes are called for by the results of standardized assessments? What do the findings of student interest or learning preference surveys suggest? In what ways do changing student demographics influence our tried and true practices? What does an analysis of students' work reveal about their particular needs? What does examination of attendance and behavior data suggest about how school is working for various groups of students? Such "data" inform our goals and guide our actions toward worthy results.

Stage 2

With specific results in mind (both student outcomes *and* professional actions), we now shift to "thinking like an assessor." Ask yourself: How will we know when we have successfully connected elements of UbD and DI? Where should we look, and what should we look for, as evidence of progress toward our goals? What "data" will provide credible evidence of targeted improvements? How will we assess our current status? What benchmarks will we examine along the way? What observable indicators will show that the UbD and DI connection is working? Having a clear assessment plan helps us clarify goals, focus actions, and inform needed adjustments to plans.

Stage 3

Mindful of clear goals and concomitant assessment evidence, it is time to think specifically about how we are going to "get there." Listed here are specific ideas for integrating UbD and DI at the classroom, school, and district levels. As you consider these possibilities, we offer a general piece of advice based on the aphorism, "Think big, start small." Recognizing that today's educators are juggling many balls, caution is advised when embarking on any change process. To avoid "innovation overload," we have found it beneficial to identify a small number of complementary actions as a starting point. Once a few changes are comfortably enacted, then others can be incorporated. Furthermore, teachers vary, just as their students do. Therefore, it is important to provide alternate routes for teachers to grow and demonstrate their growth with elements of UbD and DI—and to provide alternative support systems to ensure their success.

As an Individual Teacher

Review the observable indicators presented earlier in this chapter. Select one or a few that you feel comfortable trying. Make a specific plan for implementing the ideas and pay attention to their effects. For example, are your students more engaged? Motivated? Producing higher-quality work? Learning more? Showing deeper understanding? Which students are moving consistently toward your desired goals? Which ones are not?

As with any innovation, you are likely to encounter some rough spots as you expand your repertoire. Be prepared to tackle the learning curve as you initiate new teaching practices and classroom routines. Like a rubber band that is stretched, there's a natural tendency to want to return to your comfort level, especially when a novel approach does not go as smoothly as you would like. Recognizing this reality, a savvy veteran teacher once told us that she follows the "three tries" rule for integrating a new strategy into her repertoire. Because most classroom changes do not go perfectly on the first try, she makes a personal contract to try an idea at least three times before deciding whether it has merit for her students. This approach enables her to work out the bugs and develop a comfort level with the strategy. We urge you to do the same.

If possible, find one or more colleagues with whom to work. Changes come more easily with opportunities to plan cooperatively and problem solve, coach each other, and celebrate successes together. Different teachers will have differing perspectives and skills to bring to the process, magnifying the progress of the group by contributing through individual strengths. Partnerships between specialists (e.g., special education, gifted education, English language learning, reading, library/media) are particularly fruitful in determining best practices for students with a variety of learning needs.

Regardless of how you proceed, always keep the desired results in sight as you persevere. They are worth it and will help you continue to move forward professionally rather than retreating to the status quo.

At the School or District Level

Listed here is a set of specific actions that educators might take to foster the UbD/DI connection at the school and district levels. The lists are not meant to be exhaustive; neither are they presented with a recommended sequence. Every educational culture is unique, and actions need to fit into context. Nevertheless, these ideas reflect actions successfully undertaken in classrooms, schools, and districts.

• Establish a study group to read and discuss this book. For a more in-depth exploration, read and discuss *Understanding by Design* (Wiggins & McTighe, 2005), *How to Differentiate Instruction in Mixed-Ability Classrooms* (Tomlinson, 2001), *The Differentiated Classroom: Responding to the Needs of All Learners* (Tomlinson, 1999), or *Fulfilling the Promise of the Differentiated Classroom: Strategies and Tools for Responsive Teaching* (Tomlinson, 2003), as appropriate for the interests and needs of individuals and small groups within the school or district.

• View and discuss one or more of the following videos on DI and UbD (all available from the Association for Supervision and Curriculum Development):

Differentiating Instruction
At Work in the Differentiated Classroom

A Visit to a Differentiated Classroom
Instructional Strategies for the Differentiated Classroom
The Common Sense of Differentiation
What Is Understanding?
Using Backward Design

• Send a representative team of teachers and administrators to local, regional, or national workshops or conferences on UbD and DI.

• Sponsor an introductory workshop on DI, UbD, or their integration within the district or school (e.g., on an in-service day).

• Explore essential questions about UbD and DI in faculty and team meetings. Start with the following questions:

How can we address standards without standardization?
What content is worth understanding?
What role does classroom environment play in learning?
How do we know that students *really* understand what we teach?
How can we use pre-assessment and ongoing assessment data to shape our teaching for maximum student success?
How can we tap into student motivation to learn in a standards-based era?
What role does culture play in shaping the school experiences of our students?
How do we raise achievement without fixating on "practice tests"?

• Send a "scout" team to visit a school or district in the region using DI and UbD, and report back on potential benefits for your school/district.

• Identify a cadre of teachers and administrators to spearhead UbD/DI integration efforts in the school/district.

• Identify a school or district planning team to review these publications and develop an action plan: *Leadership for Differentiating Schools and Classrooms* (Tomlinson & Allan, 2000) and *Differentiated Instruction Stage 2: An ASCD Professional Development Planner* (Association for Supervision and Curriculum Development, 2003).

• Provide time and other incentives for the cadre to design and share differentiated UbD units.

• Create teams of differentiation specialists (e.g., a special education teacher, a Chapter I teacher, a gifted education teacher, and a teacher of

English language learners) who meet regularly to share ideas from their specialties so that they are increasingly comfortable addressing varied learner needs, and who have schedules that place them regularly in general education classrooms to do so.

- Conduct focused faculty meetings (e.g., monthly) to share one specific idea for integrating UbD and DI.
- Offer incentive grants to teams or schools interested in exploring the integration of UbD and DI.
- Work in grade-level or department groups to unpack content standards (i.e., identify understandings and essential questions).
- Work in grade-level or department groups to develop core performance tasks with differentiated options and common scoring rubrics.
- Work in grade-level or department groups to discuss implementation of flexible instructional routines that allow for attention to small groups and individuals.
- Analyze disaggregated achievement data to identify targeted areas needing differentiated instruction.
- Analyze current achievement data to identify areas of student misunderstanding and develop intervention plans.
- Create a school/district UbD curriculum map (i.e., containing understandings, essential questions, and core performance tasks).
- Develop a list of key indicators for quality application of UbD and DI for use in walkthroughs.
- Sponsor a three- to five-day summer curriculum design/differentiated instruction workshops within the district (or partner with a neighboring district).
- Develop and implement a three- to five-year action plan for staff and curriculum development on DI and UbD.
- Develop and implement a new teacher induction program around UbD and DI.
- Work in grade-level or department groups to review and evaluate student work on core performance tasks. Select school- or districtwide "anchors" for the common rubrics.
- Establish and implement action research/lesson study teams around achievement problem areas.

- Develop a standards-based grading and reporting system that includes progress and work habit categories.
- Revise the teacher/administrative appraisal process based on DI and UbD.
- Seek state, federal, and foundation grants to support UbD and DI implementation.

The possibilities are many for moving ahead with classrooms whose hallmarks are high-quality curriculum and instruction that work for each learner. The challenges are many as well. In the end, as is typically the case in education, progress stems from the informed and persistent efforts of those educators who understand that yesterday is never good enough for tomorrow. They are like the airline that announced a prestigious award by declaring, "We've just been named the nation's number one airline—and we promise to do better." For those educators, we believe the combination of UbD and DI is a worthy guide for the journey.

APPENDIX

As educators, we should look for practices grounded in scholarship. Our profession, like all other professions, strengthens as we engage in the cycle of examining practice, developing theory, and systematically investigating both theory and practice.

This appendix provides an overview of the theory, research, and expert advice in support of teaching for understanding and responsive instruction.

Support for Understanding by Design in Theory and Research

The Understanding by Design framework is guided by the confluence of evidence from two streams: theoretical research in cognitive psychology and results of student achievement studies.

Research in Cognitive Psychology

We begin by examining a comprehensive synthesis of findings over years of research in learning and cognition, summarized in a comprehensive yet readable fashion in *How People Learn: Brain, Mind, Experience, and School* (National Research Council, 2000). That book offers new conceptions of the learning process and explains how skill and understanding in key subjects are most effectively acquired.

Key findings relevant to Understanding by Design include the following:

173

• Views on effective learning have shifted from a focus on the benefits of diligent drill and practice to a focus on students' understanding and application of knowledge.

• Learning must be guided by generalized principles to be widely applicable. Knowledge learned at the level of rote memory rarely transfers; transfer most likely occurs when the learner knows and understands underlying concepts and principles that can be applied to problems in new contexts. Learning with understanding is more likely to promote transfer than simply memorizing information from a text or a lecture.

• Experts seek to develop an understanding of problems, which often involves thinking in terms of core concepts or big ideas. Novices' knowledge is much less likely to be organized around big ideas; novices are more likely to approach problems by searching for correct formulas and pat answers that fit their everyday intuitions.

• Research on expertise suggests that superficial coverage of many topics in the domain may be a poor way to help students develop the competencies that will prepare them for future learning and work. Curricula that emphasize breadth of knowledge may prevent effective organization of knowledge because there is not enough time to learn anything in depth. Curricula that are "a mile wide and an inch deep" run the risk of developing disconnected rather than connected knowledge.

• Feedback is fundamental to learning, but feedback opportunities are limited in many classrooms. Students may receive grades on tests and essays, but these are summative assessments that occur at the end of learning segments. Grades, by themselves, do not provide the specific and timely information needed for improvement. What is needed are formative assessments, which provide students with opportunities to revise and improve the quality of their thinking and understanding.

• Many assessments measure only propositional (factual) knowledge and never ask whether students know when, where, and why to use that knowledge. Given the goal of learning with understanding, assessments and feedback must focus on understanding and not simply on memory for procedures or facts.

• Expert teachers know the structure of their disciplines, and this knowledge provides them with cognitive road maps that guide the assignments that they give students, the assessments that they use to gauge student progress, and the questions that they ask in the give and take of classroom life. The point is that teaching consists only of a set of general methods, that a good teacher can teach any subject, and that content knowledge alone is sufficient.

These findings provide a conceptual base for specific instruction and assessment practices approaches in Understanding by Design.

Studies of Student Achievement

The following section summarizes the results of three achievement studies. Though differing somewhat in subject area and grade levels, the findings are consistent in their support for the principles and practices of Understanding by Design.

Newmann, Bryk, and Nagoka (2001) investigated 24 restructured schools at the elementary, middle, and high school levels to study the effects of authentic pedagogy and assessment approaches in mathematics and social studies. Authentic pedagogy and assessment approaches were measured by a set of standards that included higher-order thinking, deep-knowledge approaches, and connections to the world beyond the classroom.

Similar students in classrooms with high and low levels of authentic pedagogy and performance were compared, and the results were striking: Students with high levels of authentic pedagogy and assessment were helped substantially whether they were high- or low-achieving students. Another significant finding was that the inequalities between high- and low-performing students were greatly decreased when normally low-performing students were taught and assessed using these strategies. These findings support Understanding by Design, which emphasizes the use of authentic performance assessments and pedagogy that promotes a focus on deep knowledge and understanding, and active and reflective teaching and learning.

Additional support emerged from two recent studies of factors influencing student achievement that were conducted in Chicago public schools through the Consortium on Chicago School Research. In the first study, Smith, Lee, and Newmann (2001) focused on the link between different forms of instruction and learning in elementary schools. Test scores from more than 100,000 students in grades 2–8 and surveys from more than 5,000 teachers in 384 Chicago elementary schools were examined. The results provide strong empirical support that the nature of the instructional approach that teachers use influences how much students learn in reading and mathematics. More specifically, the study found clear and consistent evidence that interactive teaching methods were associated with more learning in both subjects. For the purposes of the study, Smith and colleagues (2001) characterized interactive instruction as follows:

> The teacher's role is primarily one of guide or coach. Teachers using this form of instruction create situations in which students . . . ask questions, develop strategies for solving problems, and communicate with one another. . . . Students are often expected to explain their answers and discuss how they arrived at their conclusions. These teachers usually assess students' mastery of knowledge through discussions, projects, or tests that demand explanation and extended writing. Besides content mastery, the process of developing the answer is also viewed as important in assessing the quality of the students' work.
>
> In classrooms that emphasize interactive instruction, students discuss ideas and answers by talking, and sometimes arguing, with each other and with the teacher. Students work on applications or interpretations of the material to develop new or deeper understandings of a given topic. Such assignments may take several days to complete. Students in interactive classrooms are often encouraged to choose the questions or topics they wish to study within an instructional unit designed by the teacher. Different students may be working on different tasks during the same class period. (p. 12)

The type of instruction found to enhance student achievement parallels methods advocated by Understanding by Design for developing and assessing student understanding.

In a related study, Newmann, Bryk, and Nagaoka (2001) examined the relationship of the nature of classroom assignments to standardized test performance. Researchers systematically collected and analyzed classroom writing and mathematics assignments in grades 3, 6, and 8 from randomly selected and control schools over the course of three years. In addition, they evaluated student work generated by the various assignments. Finally, the researchers examined correlations among the nature of classroom assignments, the quality of student work, and scores on standardized tests. Assignments were rated according to the degree to which they required "authentic" intellectual work, which the researchers described as follows:

> Authentic intellectual work involves original application of knowledge and skills, rather than just routine use of facts and procedures. It also entails disciplined

inquiry into the details of a particular problem and results in a product or presentation that has meaning or value beyond success in school. We summarize these distinctive characteristics of authentic intellectual work as construction of knowledge, through the use of disciplined inquiry, to produce discourse, products, or performances that have value beyond school. (pp. 14–15)

This study concluded:

> Students who received assignments requiring more challenging intellectual work also achieved greater than average gains on the Iowa Tests of Basic Skills in reading and mathematics, and demonstrated higher performance in reading, mathematics, and writing on the Illinois Goals Assessment Program. Contrary to some expectations, we found high-quality assignments in some very disadvantaged Chicago classrooms and [found] that all students in these classes benefited from exposure to such instruction. We conclude, therefore, [that] assignments calling for more authentic intellectual work actually improve student scores on conventional tests. (p. 29)[1]

Educators familiar with Understanding by Design will immediately recognize the parallels. The instructional methods that were found to enhance student achievement are basic elements of the pedagogy in the UbD planning model. As in the researchers' conception of "authentic" intellectual work, UbD instructional approaches call for the student to construct meaning through disciplined inquiry. Assessments of understanding call for students to apply their learning in "authentic" contexts and explain or justify their work.

The Third International Mathematics and Science Study (TIMSS), conducted in 1995, tested mathematics and science achievement of students in 42 countries at three grade levels (4, 8, and 12) and was the largest and most comprehensive and rigorous assessment of its kind ever undertaken. Although the outcomes of TIMSS are well known—American students are outperformed by students in most other industrialized countries (Martin, Mullis, Gregory, Hoyle, & Shen, 2000)—the results of the less-publicized companion TIMSS teaching study offer explanatory insights. In an exhaustive analysis of classroom teaching in the United States, Japan, and Germany using videotapes, surveys, and test data, researchers present striking evidence of the benefits of teaching for understanding in optimizing performance.[2] For example, data from the TIMSS tests and instructional studies clearly show that, although the Japanese teach fewer topics in mathematics, their students achieve better results. Rather than "covering" many discrete skills, Japanese teachers state that their primary aim is to develop conceptual understanding in their students. They emphasize depth versus superficial coverage; that is, although they cover less ground in terms of discrete topics or pages in a textbook, they emphasize problem-based learning, in which rules and theorems are derived and explained by the students, thus leading to deeper understanding (Stigler & Hiebert, 1999). This approach reflects what UbD describes as "uncovering" the curriculum. In summary, nations with higher test scores use teaching and learning strategies that promote understanding rather than "coverage" and rote learning.

Recognition of the theoretical and practical virtues of the Understanding by Design framework has led numerous schools, districts, regional service agencies, universities, and other educational organizations to use UbD in their work:

• Intel's Teach for the Future Program incorporates UbD in its national teacher training program.

• The John F. Kennedy Center for the Performing Arts CETA program (Changing Education Through the Arts) coordinates a multischool and multidistrict curriculum project for designing interdisciplinary units featuring infusion of the arts. The resulting products are based on the UbD framework and shared through the UbD Web site (http://www.ubdexchange.org).

• With funding from the Bill and Melinda Gates Foundation, the state of Washington is using the Understanding by Design framework as a cornerstone in its training for teacher leaders on curriculum and assessment design. Over the past three years, more than 3,000 teachers have participated in this systematic statewide training.

• The International Baccalaureate program used the UbD framework to redesign the template for its Primary Years Program (PYP), a curriculum used worldwide.

• The Peace Corps has adopted UbD as a framework to guide both its international curriculum development (e.g., Worldwide Schools) and its general training for Peace Corps volunteers.

• National Science Foundation–funded middle school science and mathematics curriculum projects selected Understanding by Design as the design format.

• The California State Leadership Academy (CSLA) used UbD as the framework for revising its comprehensive statewide leadership-training curriculum.

• The Corporation for Public Broadcasting, in partnership with the Annenberg Foundation, has produced an eight-volume videotape series, *The Arts in Every Classroom*. Programs 5 and 6, "Designing Multi-Arts Curriculum" and "The Role of Assessment in Curriculum Design," illustrate the use of UbD for curriculum and assessment development in the arts.

• The Texas Social Studies Center adopted UbD as the curriculum framework used in developing model, standards-based units for statewide dissemination. Information is available at http://www.tea.state.tx.us/ssc/ubd.html.

Support for Differentiated Instruction in Theory and Research

This section examines the theory and research base for differentiated instruction. You will note that both UbD and DI draw on the same base of cognitive psychology and human development and thus suggest complementary practices.

Beyond the commonsense and experiential reasons for advocating instruction that is responsive to learner need, a body of theory and research clarifies the underpinnings of differentiation and its effects on learning. That body of theory and research is summarized here. (For a more detailed examination of that theory and research, as well as challenges of implementing responsive instruction, see Tomlinson et al., 2004.)

Students differ in readiness, interest, and learning profile. Although the three factors overlap and intersect, it is clarifying to examine each one separately. The significance of the elements in learning and effects of responding to student variance in each element provides a framework for examining theory and research.

Readiness

Readiness has to do with a student's proximity to or proficiency with particular knowledge, understanding, and skill. Readiness affects a student's growth as a learner. The theoretical line of logic that supports differentiation is as follows:

• Learners must work at an appropriate degree of challenge or degree of difficulty with what they seek to learn.

• When tasks are too difficult for students, they become frustrated and do not learn effectively or efficiently.

• When tasks are too easy for students, they become bored and do not learn—in spite of the fact that they might earn high grades.

• To learn, tasks for a student must be moderately challenging for that particular student.

• Learning happens when a task is a little too difficult for a learner and scaffolding is provided to help the student span the difficulty.

• Learning occurs through a progression of appropriately scaffolded tasks at degrees of difficulty just beyond a particular student's reach.

• Motivation to learn is decreased when tasks are consistently too difficult or too easy for a learner (Csikszentmihalyi, Rathunde, & Whalen, 1993; Howard, 1994; Jensen, 1998; National Research Council, 2000; Vygotsky, 1962, 1978).

Also in regard to readiness, a number of research studies over an extended period of time continue to suggest benefits when tasks match learner readiness, including these findings:

• Students learn more effectively when teachers diagnose a student's skill level and prescribe appropriate tasks (Fisher et al., 1980).

• Students learn more effectively when a task structure matches a student's level of development (Hunt, 1971).

• In classrooms where individual students worked at a high success rate, they felt better about themselves and the subjects they were studying, and also learned more (Fisher et al., 1980).

• Students in multigrade classrooms, where differentiation is both an intent and a necessity, outperform students in single-grade classrooms on 75 percent of measures used (Miller, 1990). Other studies show benefits to students in multigrade classrooms compared to single-grade classrooms in terms of study habits, social interaction, cooperation, and attitude toward school. They also scored as well as or better than single-grade counterparts on achievement tests (Gayfer, 1991).

• In a study of 57 nongraded classrooms, achievement results favored the nongraded classrooms in 58 percent of settings reviewed, found nongraded classrooms at least as effective as graded ones in 33 percent of settings reviewed, and favored graded classrooms in only 9 percent of settings reviewed. Mental health components favored the nongraded classrooms as well. Furthermore, indications are that effects become more positive the longer students stay in such settings (Anderson & Pavan, 1993).

• In a five-year longitudinal study of adolescents, students whose skills were underchallenged by tasks demonstrated low involvement in learning activities and lessening of concentration. Students whose skills were inadequate for the level of challenge required by tasks demonstrated both low achievement and a diminished sense of self-worth. The researchers concluded that teachers who were effective in developing student talent created tasks commensurate with student skills (Csikszentmihalyi et al., 1993).

Interest

Interest has to do with a student's proclivity for and engagement with a topic or area of study. Interest affects a student's motivation to learn. Among the theoretical underpinnings of differentiation in response to student interest are these principles and the theorists who propose them:

• When an individual's interest is tapped, learning is more likely to be rewarding and the student more likely to become an autonomous learner (Bruner, 1961).

• By helping students discover and pursue interests, we can maximize their engagement with learning, their productivity, and their individual talents (Amabile, 1983; Collins & Amabile, 1999).

• When students feel a sense of "flow" with their work, they are more likely to work hard, to work in a sustained fashion, and to want to develop the skills necessary to complete the work (Csikszentmihalyi, 1990).

Among research findings that suggest the importance of addressing students' interests in the classroom are the following:

• The freedom to choose what to work on, questions to pursue, and topics for study lays the groundwork for creative achievement (Collins & Amabile, 1999).

• Student motivation can be maintained over time if teachers engage students in discussing the pleasure of their work in environments where learners feel free to exchange ideas and share interests (Hennessey & Zbikowski, 1993).

• Student interest is key to ongoing student motivation to pursue tasks at increasing levels of complexity, and satisfaction with earlier tasks is often important in keeping students engaged with work that is temporarily not interesting to them (Csikszentmihalyi, 1990).

• When students are interested in what they study, there are positive influences on learning in both the short and long term (Hébert, 1993; Renninger, 1990).

Learning Profile

Learning profile refers to preferred modes of learning or ways in which students will best process what they need to learn. Learning profile is shaped by a person's gender, culture, learning style, and intelligence preference. These shaping factors often overlap. Learning profile influences efficiency of learning. Among the theoretical underpinnings of differentiation in response to student learning profile are these principles and the theorists who propose them:

• Various classroom features, including environmental, emotional, sociological, and physical features, can influence both student attitude about learning and learning itself (Dunn, 1996).

• Students' own neurological patterns—such as attention control, memory systems, language systems, sequential and spatial ordering systems, motor systems, higher-order thinking systems, and social thinking systems—affect how they learn. When a classroom is a mismatch for a student's needs, that student is likely to struggle in school (Levine, 2002).

• Intelligence manifests itself in a variety of spheres. Even though these manifestations are fluid rather than fixed, there is benefit to addressing a learner's intelligence preferences in instruction (Gardner, 1983; Sternberg, 1985).

• A person's gender can influence the way that person sees and inter-acts with the world—including the classroom. Although generalizing to a particular gender is *not* appropriate, there are likely some female-preferred learning patterns and some male-preferred learning patterns (Gilligan, 1982; Gurian, 2001; Tannen, 1990).

• A person's culture shapes his or her perspectives, points of view, frames of reference, modes of communication, sense of identity, and cogni-tive style. Although any culture demonstrates great variance, and it is not appropriate to generalize to a culture, classrooms that favor cultural patterns of one group and are inhospitable to those of other groups are likely to have negative effects on the learning of students from the nonfavored groups (Banks, 1993, 1994; Delpit, 1995; Lasley & Matczynski, 1997). Particular classrooms may also be more beneficial to students from some economic classes than from others (Garcia, 1995). It is important for classrooms to provide a range of materials, processes, and procedures for learning so that students from many backgrounds find them comfortable and effective places to learn (Educational Research Service, 2003).

Among research findings that suggest the importance of addressing students' learning profile needs in the classroom are:

• A meta-analysis of research on the effects of learning style accommo-dation in the classroom found significant attitude and achievement gains for students from a wide range of cultural groups (Sullivan, 1993).

• Dunn and Griggs (1995) report positive learning effects through addressing students' learning profiles for elementary students, secondary students, students with emotional difficulties, and students with learning disabilities—as well as for Native American, Hispanic, African American, Asian American, and Caucasian students.

• When students' cultural differences are ignored or misunderstood in the classroom, the academic success of students from many minority groups is likely to be undermined (Delpit, 1995).

• Students at the primary, elementary, middle, and high school levels have achieved significantly better than peers in control groups when class-room instruction was matched to their preferred learning patterns (i.e., ana-lytical, creative, or practical). This was even the case when students were taught through their preferences and tested conventionally (Grigorenko & Sternberg, 1997; Sternberg, 1997; Sternberg, Torff, & Grigorenko, 1998).

Looking at the Differentiation Model as a Whole

A new and growing body of research is looking at the impact of applying differentiation as a model of instruction in classrooms. Among those studies and their findings are these:

• Across classrooms in a number of schools, achievement and attitude-about-school benefits accrued to low-economic primary grade students who were taught in accordance with identified "intelligence preferences" (Tomlinson, Callahan, & Lelli, 1997).

• Middle school students in a differentiation treatment group in five schools showed small but statistically significant achievement gains when compared with control classrooms and assessment treatment classrooms (Brighton, Hertberg, Callahan, Tomlinson, & Moon, in press).

• Elementary students with a pattern of low achievement on high-stakes standardized tests had strong and significant achievement results in a differentiated classroom (Brimijoin, 2002).

• Students at all levels of performance in an elementary school in which teachers have studied and applied principles of differentiation over a four-year period have continued to demonstrate positive achievement gains compared to achievement gains in other schools in the same district over the same period (Tomlinson, 2005).

• Students in a high school where principles of differentiation have been studied and applied by teachers over three years demonstrate achievement gains (Tomlinson, 2005).

Research related to differentiation and student benefit is encouraging, but it is important to note that we need many more studies to indicate which elements of differentiation do or do not benefit particular students and to what degree and under what circumstances benefits do or do not accrue. We also need to add to a developing body of research on factors that encourage and discourage teachers in attending to student differences. Each teacher and each school has not only the capacity but the responsibility not only to apply particular models of teaching but also to study carefully the results of such implementation on their own students.

Calls for Differentiated Classrooms

Based on both research and the realities of contemporary classrooms, admonitions to teach with student variance in mind are expressed from many areas of educational practice these days.

• Speaking to teachers of young children, the National Association for the Education of Young Children (NAEYC) reminds us that it is the responsibility of schools to adjust to children's developmental needs and levels rather than expecting children to adapt to an educational system that fails to address their individual needs and development (LaParo, Pianta, & Cox, 2000).

• Addressing teachers of adolescents, *Turning Points 2000* (Jackson & Davis, 2000) advises that classes should be composed of learners of diverse needs, achievement levels, interests, and approaches to learning, and that instruction should be differentiated to take advantage of the diversity, not ignore it.

• Focusing on high school teachers, researchers counsel that high school classrooms need to provide a range of opportunities for success for varied learners and to adjust modes of teaching to individuals' backgrounds, talents, interests, and needs indicated by past performance (Darling-Hammond, Ancess, & Ort, 2002).

• Looking at successful reading instruction, we are told that exemplary teachers don't use scripted, one-size-fits-all instructional materials. Such teachers teach students, not programs. These teachers focus on engaging individuals with reading and writing in the content areas (Allington, 2003).

• Defining professional teaching, the National Board for Professional Teaching Standards (1989) states as its first proposition that excellent teachers will recognize individual differences in their students and adjust their practice accordingly.

• Exploring the relationship between assessment and instruction, and uses of assessment to promote learning, Earl (2003) says:

> Differentiation doesn't mean a different program for each student in the class, and it doesn't mean ability grouping to reduce the differences. It means using what you know about learning and about each student to improve your teaching so that students all work in ways that have an optimal effect on their learning. And assessment provides the necessary information to do it. (p. 87)

Earl also reminds us that once we have a sense of what a particular student needs in order to learn, differentiation is no longer an option but rather an obvious response on the part of the teacher. This line of thought captures much of the shared intent of DI and UbD. It proposes that we should have clear educational goals in mind, consistently assess to find out where particular students are in their progression toward those goals, and use the assessment data to ensure that we support each student in achieving success in ways that work for that particular student. To do this, Earl suggests, is a professional responsibility.

Reflecting the comments of students he has studied, Sarason (1990) reminds all teachers that students feel betrayed by a one-size-fits-all delivery system demanding that everyone learn the same thing at the same time in the same way, no matter what their individual needs may be. The students, he reports, are asking for a different approach to teaching and learning.

Notes

1. The complete research reports are available online at http://www.consortium-chicago.org/publications/piv001.html.
2. Additional information about this significant research may be found on the TIMSS Web site (http://nces.ed.gov/timss/).

REFERENCES

Adler, M. J. (1982). *The Paideia proposal: An educational manifesto.* New York: Macmillan.

Allington, R. (2003). The schools we have, the schools we need. Retrieved September 11, 2003, from http://cela.albany.edu/schools/rtinvite.html.

Amabile, T. (1983). *The social psychology of creativity.* New York: Springer.

Anderson, R., & Pavan, B. (1993). *Nongradedness: Helping it to happen.* Lancaster, PA: Technomic.

Association for Supervision and Curriculum Development. (2003). *Differentiated instruction stage 2: An ASCD professional development planner.* Alexandria, VA: Author.

Banks, J. (1993). *Multicultural education: Issues and perspectives* (2nd ed.). Boston: Allyn & Bacon.

Banks, J. (1994). *Multiethnic education: Theory and practice* (3rd ed.). Boston: Allyn & Bacon.

Black, P., & William, D. (1998). Inside the black box: Raising standards for classroom assessment. *Phi Delta Kappan, 80*(2), 139–148.

Bloom, B. S. (Ed.). (1956). *Taxonomy of educational objectives: The classification of educational goals: Handbook I. Cognitive domain.* New York: Longmans, Green.

Bransford, J., Brown, A. L., & Cocking, R. R. (2000). *How people learn: Brain, mind, experience, and school (expanded edition).* Washington, DC: National Research Council.

Bransford, J., Brown, A. L., Cocking, R. R., & National Research Council (U.S.), Committee on Developments in the Science of Learning. (1999). *How people learn: Brain, mind, experience, and school.* Washington, DC: National Academy Press.

Brighton, C., Hertberg, H., Callahan, C., Tomlinson, C., & Moon, T. (In press). *The feasibility of high end learning in academically diverse middle schools.* Storrs, CT: National Research Center on the Gifted and Talented.

Brimijoin, K. (2002). *Expertise in differentiation: A preservice and inservice teacher make their way.* Unpublished doctoral dissertation, University of Virginia, Charlottesville, VA.

Bruner, J. (1961). The act of discovery. *Harvard Educational Review, 31,* 21–32.

Collins, M., & Amabile, T. (1999). Motivation and creativity. In R. J. Sternberg (Ed.), *Handbook of creativity* (pp. 297–312). New York: Cambridge University Press.

Costa, A., & Kallick, B. (2000). *Discovering and exploring habits of mind.* Alexandria, VA: Association for Supervision and Curriculum Development.

Costa, A., & Kallick, B. (2000). *Activating and engaging habits of mind.* Alexandria, VA: Association for Supervision and Curriculum Development.

Covey, S. (1989). *Seven habits of highly effective people: Restoring the character ethic.* New York: Simon & Schuster.

Csikszentmihalyi, M. (1990). *Flow: The psychology of optimal experience.* New York: Harper & Row.

Csikszentmihalyi, M., Rathunde, K. R., & Whalen, S. (1993). *Talented teenagers: The roots of success and failure.* New York: Cambridge University Press.

Darling-Hammond, L., Ancess, J., & Ort, S. W. (2002). Reinventing high school: Outcomes of the Coalition Campus Schools Project. *American Educational Research Journal, 39*(3), 639–673.

Day, H. I., Berlyne, D. E., Hunt, D. E., & Ontario Institute for Studies in Education, Department of Applied Psychology. (1971). *Intrinsic motivation: A new direction in education.* Toronto: Holt.

Delpit, L. (1995). *Other people's children: Cultural conflict in the classroom.* New York: New Press.

Dunn, R. (1996). *How to implement and supervise a learning styles program.* Alexandria, VA: Association for Supervision and Curriculum Development.

Dunn, R., & Griggs, S. (1995). *Multiculturalism and learning style: Teaching and counseling adolescents.* Westport, CT: Praeger.

Earl, L. M. (2003). *Assessment as learning: Using classroom assessment to maximize student learning.* Thousand Oaks, CA: Corwin.

Educational Research Service. (2003). *What we know about culture and learning.* Arlington, VA: Author.

Erickson, L. (1998). *Concept-based curriculum and instruction.* Thousand Oaks, CA: Corwin.

Fisher, C., Berliner, D., Filby, N., Marliave, R., Cahen, L., & Dishaw, M. (1980). Teaching behaviors, academic learning time, and student achievement: An overview. In C. Denham & A. Lieberman (Eds.), *Time to learn* (pp. 7–32). Washington, DC: National Institutes of Education.

Flavell, J. (1985). *Cognitive development.* Englewood Cliffs, NJ: Prentice Hall.

Garcia, G. (1995). Equity challenges in authentically assessing students from diverse backgrounds. *Educational Forum, 59*(1), 64–73.

Gardner, H. (1983). *Frames of mind: The theory of multiple intelligences.* New York: Basic Books.

Gayfer, M. (1991). *The multi-grade classroom: Myth and reality, a Canadian study.* Toronto: Canadian Education Association.

Gilligan, C. (1982). *In a different voice: Psychological theory and women's development.* Cambridge, MA: Harvard University Press.

Grigorenko, E., & Sternberg, R. (1997). Styles of thinking, abilities, and academic performance. *Exceptional Children, 63*, 295–312.

Gurian, M. (2001). *Boys and girls learn differently: A guide for teachers and parents.* San Francisco: Jossey-Bass.

Guskey, T. (2000). Grading policies that work against standards . . . and how to fix them. *NASSP Bulletin, 84*(620), 28.

Guskey, T., & Bailey, J. (2001). *Developing grading and reporting systems for student learning.* Thousand Oaks, CA: Corwin.

Hébert, T. (1993). Reflections at graduations: The long-term impact of elementary school experiences in creative productivity. *Roeper Review, 16*(1), 22–28.

Hendrie, C. (2002). Errors on tests in Nevada and Georgia cost publisher Harcourt. *Education Week, 22*(1), 24.

Hennessey, B., & Zbikowski, S. (1993). Immunizing children against the negative effects of reward: A further examination of intrinsic motivation training techniques. *Creativity Research Journal, 6,* 297–307.

Howard, P. (1994). *An owner's manual for the brain.* Austin, TX: Leorian.

Hunt, D. E. (1971). *Matching models in education* [Monograph No. 10]. Ontario, Canada: Institute for Studies in Education.

Jackson, A., & Davis, G. (2000). *Turning points 2000: Educating adolescents in the 21st century.* New York: Teachers College Press.

Jensen, E. (1998). *Teaching with the brain in mind.* Alexandria, VA: Association for Supervision and Curriculum Development.

Kameenui, E. J., Carnine, D. W., Dixon, R. C., Simmons, D. C., & Coyne, M. D. (2002). *Effective teaching strategies that accommodate diverse learners* (2nd ed.). Upper Saddle River, NJ: Merrill/ Prentice Hall.

Kean, M. (1994). *Criteria for a good assessment system.* Proceedings of the 1994 National Association of Test Directors Annual Symposium, presented at the National Council on Measurement in Education Annual Conference, New Orleans, LA.

Knapp, M. S., Shields, P. , & Turnbull, B. J. (1992). *Academic challenge for children of poverty: The summary report.* Arlington, VA: Educational Research Service.

LaParo, K., Pianta, R., & Cox, M. (2000). Teachers' reported transition practices for children transitioning into kindergarten and first grade. *Exceptional Children, 67*(1), 7–20.

Lasley, T., & Matczynski, T. (1997). *Strategies for teaching in a diverse society: Instructional models.* Belmont, CA: Wadsworth.

Levine, M. (2002). *A mind at a time.* New York: Simon & Schuster.

Martin, M., Mullis, I., Gregory, K., Hoyle, C., & Shen, C. (2000). *Effective schools in science and mathematics: IEA's third international math and science study.* Boston: International Study Center, Lynch School of Education, Boston College.

Marzano, R. (1992). *A different kind of classroom: Teaching with dimensions of learning.* Alexandria, VA: Association for Supervision and Curriculum Development.

Marzano, R., & Kendall, J. (1998). *Content knowledge.* Aurora, CO: Mid-continent Regional Educational Laboratory.

McTighe, J., & Seif, E. (2002). *Observable indicators of teaching or understanding.* Available online: http://www.ubdexchange.org.

McTighe, J., & Wiggins, G. (2004). *The Understanding by Design professional development workbook.* Alexandria, VA: Association for Supervision and Curriculum Development.

Miller, B. (1990). A review of the quantitative research on multigrade instruction. *Research in Rural Education, 7,* 3–12.

National Board for Professional Teaching Standards. (1989). *What teachers should know and be able to do.* Available online: http://www.nbpts.org/about/coreprops.cfm#introfcp (accessed December 28, 2004).

Newmann, F., Bryk, A., Nagaoka, J. (2001). *Authentic intellectual work and standardized tests: Conflict or coexistence.* Chicago: Consortium on Chicago School Research.

Nickerson, R. (1989). New directions in educational assessment (Interview on assessment issues with Lori Shepard). *Phi Delta Kappan, 70*(9), 680–697.

O'Connor, K. (2002). *How to grade for learning: Linking grades to standards.* Arlington Heights, IL: Skylight.

Reeves, D. (2002). *Making standards work.* Englewood, CA: Center for Performance Assessment.

Renninger, K. (1990). Children's play interests, representations, and activity. In R. Fivush & Hudson, J. (Eds.), *Knowing and remembering in young children* (Emory Cognition Series, Vol. 3, pp. 127–165). New York: Cambridge University Press.

Sarason, S. (1990). *The predictable failure of educational reform: Can we change course before it's too late?* San Francisco: Jossey-Bass.

Smith, J., Lee, V., & Newmann, F. (2001). *Instruction and achievement in Chicago elementary schools.* Chicago: Consortium on Chicago School Research.

Sternberg, R. (1985). *Beyond IQ: A triarchic theory of human intelligence.* New York: Cambridge University Press.

Sternberg, R. (1997). What does it mean to be smart? *Educational Leadership, 55*(7), 20–24.

Sternberg, R., Torff, B., & Grigorenko, E. (1998). Teaching triarchically improves student achievement. *Journal of Educational Psychology, 90,* 374–385.

Stigler, J. W., & Hiebert, J. (1999). *The teaching gap: Best ideas from the world's teachers for improving education in the classroom.* New York: Free Press.

Sullivan, M. (1993). *A meta-analysis of experimental research studies based on the Dunn and Dunn learning styles model and its relationship to academic achievement and performance.* Unpublished doctoral dissertation, St. John's University, Jamaica, NY.

Taba, H., & Elkins, D. (1966). *Teaching strategies for the culturally disadvantaged.* Chicago: Rand McNally.

Tannen, D. (1990). *You just don't understand: Women and men in conversation.* New York: Ballantine.

Tomlinson, C. (1999). *The differentiated classroom: Responding to the needs of all learners.* Alexandria, VA: Association for Supervision and Curriculum Development.

Tomlinson, C. (2001). *How to differentiate instruction in mixed-ability classrooms* (2nd ed.). Alexandria, VA: Association for Supervision and Curriculum Development.

Tomlinson, C. (2003). *Fulfilling the promise of the differentiated classroom: Strategies and tools for responsive teaching.* Alexandria, VA: Association for Supervision and Curriculum Development.

Tomlinson, C. (2005, November 18). Differentiated instruction as a way to achieve equity and excellence in today's schools. Presentation at Canadian Teachers' Federation Conference on Building Inclusive Schools, Ottawa, Ontario.

Tomlinson, C., & Allan, S. D. (2000). *Leadership for differentiating schools and classrooms.* Alexandria, VA: Association for Supervision and Curriculum Development.

Tomlinson, C., Brighton, C., Hertberg, H., Callahan, C., Moon, T., Brimijoin, K., Conover, L., & Reynolds, T. (2004). Differentiating instruction in response to student readiness, interest, and learning profile in academically diverse classrooms: A review of literature. *Journal for the Education of the Gifted, 27,* 119–145.

Tomlinson, C., Callahan, C., & Lelli, K. (1997). Challenging expectations: Case studies of high-potential, culturally diverse young children. *Gifted Child Quarterly, 41*(2), 5–17.

Tyler, R. (1949). *Basic principles of curriculum and instruction.* Chicago: University of Chicago Press.

Vygotsky, L. (1962). *Thought and language.* Cambridge, MA: The MIT Press.

Vygotsky, L. (1978). *Mind in society: The development of higher psychological processes.* Cambridge, MA: Harvard University Press.

White, K. (1999). Test company apologizes for N.Y.C. summer school mix-up. *Education Week, 19*(3), 8.

Wiggins, G. (1998). *Educative assessment: Designing assessments to inform and improve student performance.* San Francisco: Jossey-Bass.

Wiggins, G., & McTighe, J. (1998). *Understanding by Design.* Alexandria, VA: Association for Supervision and Curriculum Development.

Wiggins, G., & McTighe, J. (2005). *Understanding by Design* (2nd ed.). Alexandria, VA: Association for Supervision and Curriculum Development.

INDEX

About the Authors

Carol Ann Tomlinson's career bridges both practice and scholarship in education. She was a classroom teacher for 21 years, teaching at the high school, middle school, and primary levels. She was instrumental in developing a language arts program designed to effectively serve a full spectrum of learners in heterogeneous middle grades classrooms. The program was piloted and funded by the Commonwealth of Virginia and demonstrated positive achievement gains for a full range of learners in such settings. During her public school career, she also served as district coordinator for programs for both struggling and advanced learners. She was named outstanding teacher at the middle school where she taught, Jaycees Outstanding Young Educator, Soroptimist Outstanding Educator, and Virginia Governor's School Outstanding Teacher. She also received the Optimist Club Achievement in Education Award and was Virginia's Teacher of the Year in 1974.

At the University of Virginia (UVA), where she is a professor of educational leadership, foundations, and policy, Tomlinson and her colleagues have researched differentiation in a variety of contexts over the past decade. Among those are preservice teachers' understanding of and ability to address student differences, the nature of the change process in schools implementing differentiation, achievement impacts of differentiation in middle school, elementary, and high school settings, and profiles of teachers whose classroom practice enhances success of students from low-economic and/or cultural minority groups. Her research and writing have received awards from the Virginia Education Research Association, the American Education Research Association, and the National Association for Gifted Children. At UVA, she teaches graduate and undergraduate students in courses on curriculum and differentiation and serves as co-director of the university's Institutes on Academic Diversity. Tomlinson was named Outstanding Professor at the University of Virginia in 2004.

Articles written by Tomlinson have appeared in many leading journals—among them *Educational Leadership, Journal for Staff Development, Education Week, Theory into Practice, National Association for Secondary School Principals Bulletin, School Administrator, Phi Delta Kappan, Middle School Journal, Research in Middle Level Education, Evaluation Practice, Exceptional Children, Journal of Learning Disabilities, Journal for the Education of the Gifted,* and *Gifted Child Quarterly.* She is author or coauthor of 10 books on differentiation and curriculum. For ASCD, she has authored *How to Differentiate Instruction in Mixed-Ability Classrooms, The Differentiated Classroom: Responding to the Needs of All Learners, Fulfilling the Promise of the Differentiated Classroom: Strategies and Tools for Responsive Teaching,* (with Susan Allan) *Leadership for Differentiating Schools and Classrooms,* (with Caroline Cunningham Eidson) *Differentiation in Practice: A Resource Guide for Differentiating Curriculum, Grades 5–9,* and (with Cindy Strickland) *Differentiation in Practice: A Resource Guide for Differentiating Curriculum, Grades 9–12.* She has also authored a Professional Inquiry Kit on Differentiation for ASCD and has served as consultant for and featured presenter in 15 ASCD videos on differentiation. Her books have been translated into eight languages.

Tomlinson works regularly with schools and school districts and presents at conferences nationally and internationally with educators who want to develop schools that are more responsive to and successful in serving academically diverse student populations. She can be reached at Curry School of Education, The University of Virginia, P.O. Box 400277, Charlottesville, VA 22904, or via e-mail at cat3y@virginia.edu.

Jay McTighe brings a wealth of experience developed during a rich and varied career in education. He served as director of the Maryland Assessment Consortium, a state collaboration of school districts working together to develop and share formative performance assessments. Prior to this position, McTighe was involved with school improvement projects at the Maryland State Department of Education. He is known for his work with thinking skills, having coordinated statewide efforts to develop instructional strategies, curriculum models, and assessment procedures for improving the quality of student thinking. McTighe also directed the development of the Instructional Framework, a multimedia database on teaching. In addition to his work at the state level, McTighe has experience at the district level in Prince George's County, Maryland, as a classroom teacher, resource specialist, and program coordinator. He also served as director of the Maryland Summer Center for Gifted and Talented Students, a statewide residential enrichment program held at St. Mary's College. McTighe has published articles in leading journals and books, including *Educational Leadership* (ASCD), *Developing Minds* (ASCD), *Thinking Skills: Concepts and Techniques* (National Education Association), and *The Developer* (National Staff Development Council). He coauthored three books on assessment, *Assessing Learning in the Classroom* (NEA), *Assessing Outcomes: Performance Assessment Using the Dimensions of Learning Model* (ASCD), and *Scoring Rubrics in the Classroom* (Corwin Press). He is coauthor, with Grant Wiggins, of *Understanding by Design Professional Development Workbook* (ASCD), *Understanding by Design Handbook* (ASCD), and other essential Understanding by Design titles with ASCD.

McTighe has an extensive background in staff development and is a regular speaker at national, state, and district conferences and workshops. He is also a featured presenter and consultant for videotape programs including *Performance Assessment in the Classroom* (Video Journal of Education), *Developing Performance Assessments* (ASCD), and *Understanding by Design* video series (tapes 1–3) (ASCD).

McTighe received his undergraduate degree from The College of William and Mary, earned a master's degree from The University of Maryland

and has completed postgraduate studies at The Johns Hopkins University. He was selected to participate in The Educational Policy Fellowship Program through the Institute for Educational Leadership in Washington, D.C. McTighe served as a member of the National Assessment Forum, a coalition of education and civil rights organizations advocating reforms in national, state, and local assessment policies and practices. He also completed a three-year term on the ASCD Publications Committee, serving as committee chair during 1994–95.

McTighe can be reached at 6581 River Run, Columbia, MD 21044-6066. Phone: (410) 531-1610. E-mail: jmctigh@aol.com. Web site: http://jaymctighe.com.

Related ASCD Resources:
Differentiated Instruction and Understanding by Design

At the time of publication, the following ASCD resources were available; for the most up-to-date information about ASCD resources, go to www.ascd.org. ASCD stock numbers are noted in parentheses.

Mixed Media
Differentiated Instruction Professional Development Planner and Resource Package, Stage 1 (#701225)
Differentiating Instruction for Mixed-Ability Classrooms Professional Inquiry Kit by Carol Ann Tomlinson (#196213)
Understanding by Design Unit Builder (#500287)

Networks
Visit the ASCD Web site (www.ascd.org) and search for "networks" for information about professional educators who have formed groups around topics like "Brain-Based Compatible Learning," "Learning and Assessment," and "Multiple Intelligences." Look in the "Network Directory" for current facilitators' addresses and phone numbers.

Online Resources
Visit ASCD's Web site (www.ascd.org) for the following professional development courses:
Differentiating Instruction by Leslie Kiernan
Understanding by Design: An Introduction by John Brown
Understanding by Design: The Backward Design Process by John Brown
Understanding by Design: The Six Facets of Understanding by John Brown

Print Products
Making the Most of Understanding by Design by John L. Brown (#103110)
Understanding by Design Professional Development Workbook by Jay McTighe and Grant Wiggins (#103056)
Understanding by Design, Expanded 2nd Edition by Grant Wiggins and Jay McTighe (#103055)
The Differentiated Classroom: Responding to the Needs of All Learners by Carol Ann Tomlinson (#199040)
Differentiation in Practice: A Resource Guide for Differentiating Curriculum, Grades K–5, by Carol Ann Tomlinson and Caroline Cunningham Eidson (#102294)
Differentiation in Practice: A Resource Guide for Differentiating Curriculum, Grades 5–9, by Carol Ann Tomlinson and Caroline Cunningham Eidson (#102293)
Differentiation in Practice: A Resource Guide for Differentiating Curriculum, Grades 9–12, by Cindy Strickland and Carol Ann Tomlinson (#104140)

Videotapes
The Understanding by Design Video Series, three tapes (#400241)
The Common Sense of Differentiation: Meeting Specific Learner Needs in the Regular Classroom Video Series, three tapes (#405138)

For more information, visit us on the World Wide Web (http://www.ascd.org), send an e-mail message to member@ascd.org, call the ASCD Service Center (1-800-933-ASCD or 703-578-9600, then press 2), send a fax to 703-575-5400, or write to Information Services, ASCD, 1703 N. Beauregard St., Alexandria, VA 22311-1714 USA.